Kenneth S. Goodman, Hans C. Olsen, Jr., Cynthia M. Colvin, and Louis F. VanderLinde are associate professors of elementary education, Wayne State University.

Mr. Goodman received his B.A. and Ed.D. degrees from the University of California, Los Angeles (1949, 1963), and his M.A. from Los Angeles State College (1953). He was formerly research and teaching assistant at U.C.L.A.

Mr. Olsen received his B.S. from Eastern Illinois State College (1950), and his M.Ed. and Ed.D. degrees from the University of Illinois (1954, 1958). He has taught at Purdue University and the University of Illinois.

Mrs. Colvin received her B.A., M.Ed., and Ed.D. from Wayne State University (1943, 1950, 1958).

Mr. VanderLinde received his B.A. and M.A. degrees from Western Michigan University (1952, 1958), and his Ed.D. from Michigan State University (1962).

Choosing Materials

To Teach Reading

Choosing Materials

To Teach Reading

by Kenneth S. Goodman, Hans C. Olsen, Jr.,
Cynthia M. Colvin, Louis F. VanderLinde

WAYNE STATE UNIVERSITY

Wayne State University Press

DETROIT *1966*

To our families

Contents

PREFACE   9

Chapter 1   PRINCIPLES AND ANALYSIS   13
             Reasons for This Book
             Problems of Choosing Reading
                 Materials
             Real Foundation of Materials
             Analysis before Selection
             Goodness of Fit
             Organization

Chapter 2   PSYCHOLOGICAL PRINCIPLES   22
             Child Development and Textbook
                 Organization
             Personality Growth through Reading
             Provision for Individual Differences
             Readiness
             Motivation and Interest
             Other Learning Principles
             Summary

Chapter 3   SOCIOCULTURAL PRINCIPLES   41
             What Children Like to Read
             Social Class and Experience
             Dialect Differences
             Role Development
             Values
             Summary

Chapter 4   EDUCATIONAL PRINCIPLES   68
             Sequence, Scope, and Integration
             Controls
             Legibility
             Associated Learnings
             Suitability
             Teachability
             Summary

Chapter 5   LINGUISTIC PRINCIPLES   89
             What Is Linguistics?
             Accuracy of Language Information
             Phonemic Considerations
             Morphemic Considerations
             Syntactic Considerations
             Intonation Considerations
             Dialect Considerations
             General Linguistic Considerations
             Summary

Chapter 6   LITERARY PRINCIPLES   113
                  (with James R. Hengoed)
             What Is Literature?
             Reading Materials Not Literature
             Instructional Materials as a Special
                  Form of Literature
             Content
             Artistic Quality
             Summary

             APPENDIX   129
             Critical Questions for Analyzing
                  and Selecting Reading
                  Materials

             SELECTED BIBLIOGRAPHY   149
             INDEX   153

Preface

Many factors place heavy pressure on those who must analyze and select reading texts and materials for the elementary school. Teachers, supervisors, and administrators have a difficult task in assembling accurate information about such materials. Publishers' descriptions and publishers' representatives tend to claim broad utility and general validity for their materials and a large number and great variety are now on the market. But ever more effective programs of reading instruction are demanded in elementary schools.

A thorough and effective job of analyzing materials requires that school people contribute much time and energy. Even then they may be inadequately prepared to deal with the many new and quite different developments in reading that have come about in the last few years. Linguistics and programmed instruction are two examples. The lack of any established, comprehensive, generally accepted criteria to guide the analyses compounds the problem. Conflicting philosophies and differences in information result in additional pressures on elementary school personnel.

In one or more of the educators roles, each of the authors has struggled with the problem of analyzing and selecting reading texts and materials. The authors know from firsthand experience that the amount of new knowledge about reading and the variety of materials now available make it difficult to rely on old standards. As faculty members of Wayne State University, department of elementary education, they have been called on with increasing frequency to help teachers and school officials grapple with this problem. Thus, this book is an outgrowth of experience and is designed to assist school people in reading instruction. Specifically, it serves four distinct purposes:

1. It provides a list and objective discussion of principles to enable elementary school practitioners to analyze reading materials effectively and efficiently.
2. It furnishes an extensive number of principles from which analysts can choose the criteria for guiding their work.
3. It supplies a great many principles and a discussion of background information related to each, and by so doing extends the horizons of the user.
4. It illustrates the necessity for the analyst of reading materials to be *fully* aware of the criteria or standards he is applying and to apply them consistently.

Teachers, supervisors, and administrators, either individually or as members of committees, will still need to make their own value decisions of approaches and techniques. The principles and discussion in this volume are intended to give them an informed and objective foundation for the alternatives they select.

This book can be used as an intensive reference by individual teachers and by text-selection committees as a source book to determine criteria, or a handbook for occasional reference by teachers, librarians, principals, or curriculum directors. It can also serve as a valuable supplementary text in reading methods and elementary school curriculum courses in teacher education.

The authors wish to acknowledge their debt to the many

students, teachers, supervisors, and administrators who, often unknowingly, have helped broaden their horizons. They also want to acknowledge the contributions of James R. Hengoed, Boston University, who assisted in the initial stages of the book's development and shared the writing of Chapter 6. They are particularly grateful for the continuing interest, encouragement, assistance, patience, and understanding of their families.

K. S. G.

H. C. O.

C. M. C.

L. F. V.

Chapter 1

Principles and Analysis

REASONS FOR THIS BOOK

The task of selecting texts and other materials to use in teaching reading is not easy. Teachers, text-selection committees, supervisors, and others charged with this task usually find it very difficult to assemble comprehensive, objective criteria for judging and comparing proposed materials.

To do a conscientious job of evaluation, school people must expend a great deal of time and energy. Even then they may not have the background to deal with new developments—such as linguistics—in reading materials, or they may not be aware of the wide range of principles that *might* assist them in selecting materials.

The purpose of this book is to provide an objective summary of principles that can enable school practitioners to judge effectively if specific reading materials are what they are claimed. An attempt has been made to include all principles that might be found in reading materials. Those who use this book will need to select from among the principles catalogued here in accordance with their own values. They must also establish the hierarchy of emphasis for the principles they select; the choice of philosophies, objectives, and methods for analyzing and selecting reading texts and materials are left to them.

The inclusion of any principle is *not* an endorsement of

the principle or a statement of its validity. Similarly, though the intention is to be inclusive, the omission of a principle should not be interpreted as an implication that it is invalid or unimportant. Rather, it is a sign that analyzing reading material is, indeed, complex.

PROBLEMS OF CHOOSING READING MATERIALS

"With all of the materials available on the market, how do we choose the best ones for our school?"

"There are four 'slow-learners' in my third-grade class. What reading materials should I use with them?"

"Our reading program needs more phonics in it. What reading materials will give our children the best program of reading instruction with special emphasis on phonics?"

"I've heard a great deal about the use of linguistics in teaching reading. Which reading materials with linguistic labels will be most effective when correlated with my present reading program? Is there a linguistic reading program that can do the whole job of teaching reading?"

"My second-graders need some supplementary reading materials that will extend and expand our present reading program. Which are best suited for this purpose?"

"I am a beginning sixth-grade teacher expected to teach reading. What teachers' manuals or other materials designed to help teachers will be of most assistance to me?"

"Our board of education has provided money to enable us to buy workbooks for the reading program. What workbooks currently available are most likely to be of greatest utility in our program?"

"There are many children in our school system who live in 'deprived neighborhoods.' What reading materials will best help them learn this important skill?"

These questions are representative of elementary school-teachers, supervisors, and administrators. They have been selected from among those asked at educational conferences, in school faculty meetings, and in casual conversations in schools, as well as in college classes.

The above questions indicate the common desire to provide the best possible program of reading instruction. They also testify to the complexity of planning, presenting, and evaluating elementary school reading, and they reveal an awareness that instructional materials are an integral part of the reading program.

Reading materials are designed to help the teacher perform certain instructional tasks. Several types of materials are available. The most prominent of these are basal series, supplementary readers, and trade books. The others include teachers' manuals, supplementary materials (charts, filmstrips, and other special media), workbooks, review materials, and tests. New forms, such as programmed materials, kits, and pre-packaged laboratories are appearing. Each of these is prepared for a specific purpose, yet each is designed to contribute to the entire instructional program of reading. All are provided for use in helping children read more effectively and are important parts of the total program.

The amount of materials designed to aid in reading instruction is increasing at an accelerating pace. New basal texts, new workbooks, new materials of all kinds are constantly entering the market.

REAL FOUNDATION OF MATERIALS

"Similarity" is the term that still best characterizes the bulk of these materials. The basic pattern of each of the types listed earlier is relatively constant and changes slowly. Within this pattern each bit of material mirrors a particular concept of an effective reading program. Points of emphasis are dictated by the author's approach to the teaching of reading, but the pattern remains firm.

While the number of materials is growing, the variety is

also increasing. New knowledge forces reappraisal and re-organization of programs and materials. Innovation brings into existence new materials that fit within the types enumerated but add new dimensions to each, and the emphases in programs and materials are almost constantly changing. Publishing practices are being transformed; competition among publishing houses is increasing as more and more materials enter the market. "Modern materials," "up-to-date materials," "new materials," "the latest thing," are frequently heard in reading circles.

A major responsibility of school practitioners is to provide the best materials available to assist them in developing reading competence. Choices must be made from among a great many possibilities, each supported by publishers' representatives, promotional literature, and samples. The apparent similarity of many of the materials compounds the difficulty, despite each publisher's effort to point up the unique characteristics of his materials. Many publishers' representatives attempt to make the materials they are selling "all things to all people" by emphasizing what each customer wants to hear. And, of course, one would hardly expect a salesman to pin-point the weaknesses of his product. Even when publishers state principles on which their materials are based, close analysis of the materials often demonstrates great inconsistency in the application of those principles. In some cases, unstated principles may turn out to be the real foundation of the materials.

The selection of certain materials rather than others must be based on which materials best reflect application of a set of principles determined by the selector. The principles may be quite extensive in scope or they may be rather limited. They are not fully articulated in all situations. The person who says, "Oh, I don't know why. I just picked this workbook," is guided by standards just as is another who can list in detail the reasons he picked a particular book. The standards or principles may not be consciously applied, but they are used nevertheless. One goal of this book is to make this a conscious deliberate process, to make the selector aware of his choices. Logically, the more complete and consistent the set of principles employed and more deliberate the process, the sounder the basis for selecting materials best suited to provide maximum assistance in reading.

ANALYSIS BEFORE SELECTION

It is actually analysis of materials that causes much of the turmoil within those who must make the choices. The various materials under consideration must be analyzed before one or more of them can be selected. Thus, each educator becomes an analyst first and later a selector of materials. As an analyst, he must study the materials from which he will make choices. He seeks to determine their strengths and weaknesses and their appropriateness under certain conditions. The principles the analyst uses determine the scope and emphasis of his analysis.

The decision to present here as many principles as possible is deliberate. No single or consistent viewpoint is represented by these principles. Neither is there an effort to provide a comprehensive *system* of principles. The purpose is to furnish as many principles as possible that might be considered important by school practitioners; maximum utility is the aim.

Under this plan, conflicts among the principles presented are to be expected. These conflicts will be pointed out but no judgments made. A deliberate decision to provide a framework of widest utility precludes prescribing a single set of principles. Objectivity is fundamental in this approach.

The basic tenets guiding the preparation of this volume dictate presenting far more principles than any analyst can accept or profitably use. A wide range of principles may bring to the attention of analysts some they may not be familiar with. Similarly, providing background information for each of these principles may cast certain of them in a new light. Analysts will also become aware that by choosing some principles they reject others. One purpose of this book is to extend the horizons of analysts concerning principles which can guide their work.

Choices must be made among the many principles. To select wisely, the individual analyst must think through the philosophy and objectives of the reading program in his school system. This presupposes a thorough familiarity with the goals of the total school program. He should know the teachers the materials are to be selected for. The professional preparation, experience, and view of reading that teachers bring to the classroom shape the way they will use reading materials. Perhaps, above all, the analyst must know the backgrounds, needs, attitudes, and interests of the children whose experiences in reading are to be enhanced by the materials. From his knowledge of these three elements—the reading program, the teachers, and the children —he knows what is mandatory, what is unimportant, and what is unacceptable in the way of materials. On the basis of the principles chosen, he is able, through analysis, to select materials most appropriate for the situation they will be used in.

The principles finally selected become the criteria by which reading materials are analyzed. By selecting certain principles rather than others, the analyst develops for himself a more or less comprehensive and consistent framework for analyzing materials. These criteria become the norm by which the analyst determines the validity of the materials.

GOODNESS OF FIT

The validity or "goodness of fit" of the instructional materials with the established criteria provides the analyst with a means for comparing the various materials and deciding which are most suitable.

Obviously, the goodness of fit will probably never be perfect. Some materials will be more valid than others for use in a particular situation. Two factors may account for much of the disparity between materials and the norm:

1. The norm is made up of several criteria. This means that often choices must be made among the various criteria. Some materials will be stronger on a particular point than others. However, the strength may be reversed on another characteristic. For example, one basal reading series may emphasize phonics, while another may present an eclectic approach. Perhaps a more difficult situation is one in which two basal series are built around linguistic reading instruction. However, one is constructed to enable the children to derive meaning from the materials from the outset of their reading program, the other stresses a consistent phoneme-grapheme relationship. The difference in both instances is of major emphasis. Since there are usually many criteria that form the standard or norm, the emphasis accorded each of them is a matter of choice by the analyst. Determining the relative validity of several materials is not an easy task.

2. Differences in philosophy and experience among educators lead them to assign different priorities to the various criteria. What is an important criterion for one educator may be much less important to another. These differences help account for the fact that a great many analysts will be something less than completely satisfied with a specific set of materials. It is probably

true, too, that the author of that set of materials is not completely happy himself with the product of his work because he has constructed it to attract the largest number of users; he has had to make choices among his own criteria and to include things which were not part of his basic approach. The validity of reading materials is always relative. The analyst must decide which of the materials most nearly fits the norm he has established.

ORGANIZATION

The principles are categorized and discussed under five arbitrary, but convenient, labels: psychological, sociocultural, educational, linguistic, and literary.

Existing knowledge about reading tends to be organized into these five categories. This system of organization is based on the preference of reading scholars, logic, and general use. The individual categories present distinctive vantage points to view reading from. The focus of each differs from the other four. For example, linguistic information provides a quite different basis for studying principles than psychological knowledge does. Each area furnishes a foundation of organized knowledge from which principles may be drawn and examined.

Obscure and seldom-used principles are called to the attention of analysts as they study these areas. Some principles that are frequently overlooked are brought to light because these areas of knowledge provide a relatively systematic frame of reference.

Other principles, commonly recognized and employed, are viewed in a more fully rounded form as a result of being considered in the context of organized areas of knowledge. Greater understanding may result from a full and meaningful summary of background information.

The areas have within them elements upon which there

is wide agreement and dimensions of much controversy. New knowledge is always emerging and none of the five is completely stable. However, some are much more stable and have played a much greater role in reading instruction than have others. Practically the whole of one area, linguistics, is quite new to elementary school reading programs.

While new developments, controversy, and restatements of position are probably best understood in the context of these five areas, they are not mutually exclusive; they overlap and are not completely separable. Perhaps the best illustration is that "interest" is integral to the chapters on psychological, sociocultural, educational, and literary principles. That the five areas are interrelated enhances their usefulness as a framework for considering principles. A better understanding of principles may be gained as the supporting assumptions and information from several areas of knowledge are brought into full focus.

Each of the five chapters is designed to stand alone, and discusses in some depth the background information essential to an understanding of the principles presented. Terminology is clarified and the view of reading and underlying assumptions involved in specific principles are outlined. Related sections in other chapters are indicated. Each section within a chapter is followed by critical questions that embody the principles discussed in that section. An appendix consists of a compilation of these critical questions from the text.

Chapter 2

Psychological
Principles

Possibly no aspect of validity has claimed the attention of textbook writers and publishers more than the psychological. The facts of child development have guided the structure and content of reading series. The potential contribution of reading to wholesome personality growth has also affected the ways in which basic readers are written. Principles derived from learning theory—readiness, motivation, and interest—are other psychological bases for choosing and organizing reading materials. Psychological validity depends on the degree to which instructional materials help reading development, are suited to varied levels of maturity and interest, and incorporate what is now known about learning.

CHILD DEVELOPMENT AND TEXTBOOK ORGANIZATION

Many authorities in reading believe there is a close relationship between patterns of human development and reading ability. Obviously, the development of language and reading takes place within the pattern of personality development. Each individual follows this pattern and goes through a somewhat similar pattern as he acquires skill in reading. Both patterns are characterized by continuity and both include a number of stages. These stages or levels are not discrete but gradually merge into one another. Statements, such as those which follow, describe general characteristics of language learning at each of three levels:

Kindergarten and first grade:

Spoken vocabulary at five years is at least 2,500 words.

Sentences at five years may contain six or eight words.

At five and six years, the child is changing from development of large muscle skills to finer muscular co-ordination as needed in reading.

The average girl at six years is approximately one year ahead of the average boy in verbal skills.

By five or six years, interests are broadening beyond immediate environment.

After five years, language and thinking grow somewhat less egocentric.

Primary grades:

Seven-year olds recognize differences before similarities.

Abstract words are used in the primary grades but are not understood completely.

Some children can read a few words before entering school; others are far from ready to begin reading.

Five- and six-year olds develop a sight vocabulary by association (picture, charts) and by use.

In the primary grades children grow in ability to see relationships, e.g., can work on main idea or sequence in a paragraph.

Learning is fairly specific so that achievements in phonics, using context, seeing cause and effect, etc., depend upon the types of instruction and materials used.

During the primary grades the child's language and reading become more influenced by the group.

After a small slow-down on entering school, vocabulary continues to grow rapidly.

Intermediate and upper grades:

Until about eight years of age boys and girls are interested in reading the same types of story, but after that age their interests diverge and become apparent at ten.

After 12 or 13 years, social interests and the demands of school homework tend to reduce free reading.

After 12 years, reading interests and activities become much more specialized and individual.

Reading becomes a valuable tool in much school work with a wide variety of materials (newspapers, magazines, reference books) in use.

Reading, speaking, writing, and listening abilities are positively related and contribute to one another.

Reading may contribute to knowledge, increase self-insight, and enhance understanding of others![*]

The summary of language development presented above describes average behavior for many children in our society. As a generalized description of language and reading behavior, it provides several clues for assessing psychological validity of reading materials.

Critical Questions:

Does the reading material reflect consideration of child development?

Are the common characteristics of each age considered in the materials?

Do the materials emphasize differences or similarities?

Is physical maturation of children considered?

Are differences between interests and rate of development between boys and girls provided for?

---

[*] David H. Russell, "Continuity in the Reading Program," *Development in and through Reading,* Sixtieth Yearbook of the National Society for the Study of Education (Chicago: University of Chicago Press, 1961), pp. 236–37.

Is there any attempt to correlate reading with other aspects of language development?

Is reading developed as a tool of learning in successively higher grades?

Placement of reading skills. Planning a developmental reading program based on typical patterns of language behavior is difficult. As yet, there is little evidence that a close relationship exists between child development and reading achievement. The placement of reading skills appears to require an analysis of the reading process itself. Do children acquire a stock of sight words before they begin to analyze words? How rapidly can children acquire new sight vocabulary? At which stage do children begin to analyze words? What is the function of meaning in the very first stages of reading?

Attempts to judge how appropriate the placement is of reading skills are often based on typical stages in language behavior. But children vary greatly in the speed they develop reading skills and in the amount of practice they require to move from one level of proficiency to another. What may be insufficient practice for slow learners may be needless repetition for gifted and superior students. Moreover, there is no conclusive proof that there is one sequence of skill development preferable to all others, or that there is a measurable step in increased difficulty most desirable in helping children move from one level to another.

Critical Questions:

How is the placement of reading skills determined?

How much and what kind of practice of reading skills is provided?

How is meaning handled in relation to reading skills in the first stages of reading instruction?

Is a stock of sight words taught before skill instruction is introduced?

Continuity in the development of skills. There is general agreement among authorities in reading instruction that continuity is desirable. Continuity insures that no gaps exist in necessary reading experience. It is possible to evaluate the degree of continuity in a reading series only after one has identified the placement of reading skills and after one has determined whether skills are introduced at appropriate times. Then one may ask whether each skill is related to those previously acquired and whether each is repeated in gradual degrees of difficulty.

Critical Questions:
Is skill instruction provided at appropriate times?
Is a planned sequence in skill instruction evident?
Is each skill presented in successively more difficult degrees?

Completeness of skill development. It is often assumed that basal readers are suitable for use at each successive stage of reading development, and that a given set of materials can provide for the development of all necessary reading skills at each level or stage. Herrick and others suggest that, although it may be possible for reading materials to be developed by a single source for all children, there is a question as to the ability of a single source to relate materials to particular groups of children or to develop a teaching sequence adequate for all children.*

If one accepts the assumption that reading texts can provide for the development of all necessary reading skills,

---

* Virgil E. Herrick, and others, "Basic Instructional Materials in Reading," *Development in and through Reading, op. cit.,* p. 169.

it should be possible to examine sets of basic reading materials to determine whether all reading skills are presented. Provisions for achievement in such important skills as word recognition, word attack, paragraph meaning, vocabulary, comprehension and interpretation, spelling, and work-study may be noted. The choice and kinds of skills included will be closely related to the authors' views of how basic reading should be taught. The omission of certain skills and the inclusion of others may be a determining factor in one's choice of a reading series.

Critical Questions:

Are all necessary skills presented fully?
  —Phonics
  —Word recognition
  —Paragraph meaning
  —Vocabulary
  —Comprehension and interpretation
  —Spelling
  —Work-study

Which skills are emphasized and which are ignored or excluded?

Does the material meet the needs of all children?

What exclusions are made?

Content to be read. The continuous process of human development suggests that gradual and systematic development of reading skills is more appropriate to the maturity of the learner than a program characterized by omissions in the acquisition of necessary reading skills. Content or substance of what is read should also be geared to the developmental sequence. One such sequence is suggested by Harris.*

---

* Albert J. Harris, "Reading and Human Development," *Development in and through Reading, op. cit.,* p. 33.

As a child grows up, he changes in many ways. Some of the significant trends in personality development are the following:

1. From helplessness to self-help with consequent reduction of frustration and fear.
2. From dependence on others to self-reliance.
3. From living in the immediate present to wider grasp of the past and future.
4. From parent-centered to peer-centered to a wide-ranging social interest.
5. From all-or-none emotional reactions to control over one's emotional responses.
6. From self-centered egotism toward satisfaction in sharing and giving.
7. From low frustration tolerance toward ability to endure tension and to function effectively despite anxiety.
8. From emotional attachment to parents to interest in the same sex during middle childhood to heterosexual responsiveness and love in adolescence and maturity.

If one accepts a typical developmental sequence as a guide to content in the basic readers, it appears that stories would center in the "here and now" in the primary grades and move toward the "far" in time and space in the intermediate and later grades. But the child's world has changed. The extensive viewing of television has been primarily responsible. Today the child is exposed to all parts of the world and, indeed, the universe. He is transported to the past and projected into the future. The horizons of his immediate world are greatly expanded. Widespread background of vicarious experience and extended interests suggest that the content of basic readers could go beyond simple stories of home and family life. Some will feel that the accepted sequence from immediate and personal experiences in the home and community to more remote topics may have to be re-evaluated. More informational stories, more emphasis on history and science may be part of newer strategies for textbook design.

Critical Questions:

Does the content of successive units in the materials reflect general tendencies in children's personality development?

Is there a sequence from near to far?

Is there a sequence from now to then?

Is there a sequence from self to others?

Is there a sequence from the family to larger social units?

Are plots involving frustration and anxiety avoided in early grades?

Does the content reflect the increased vicarious experience of modern children?

Are nonfiction materials included to tap the broader interest of today's children?

PERSONALITY GROWTH THROUGH READING

Reading, viewed as a developmental task, occupies an important place in the child's life and affects his future achievement. By definition, developmental tasks are those which, if successfully achieved, lead to happiness and success with later tasks. The entire educational career of the child is bound up with early success or failure in reading. There is a substantial relationship between reading and school achievement and, eventually, between reading and general achievement. Success in school determines, to a certain degree, one's occupation and even the cultural group one may belong to. Therefore, learning to read has important implications for personal growth.

Many educational psychologists believe that a child's

earliest efforts should be rewarded by success. For some, this means a young child must successfully obtain meaning from the printed or written symbol. According to this viewpoint, textbooks should emphasize meaningful phrases and patterns of thought even at the earliest stages and thus facilitate the process of learning to read. How this can be done without sacrificing the values of a sharply restricted beginning vocabulary is a realistic problem for textbook writers. Another view, which appears frequently, is that success can be attained through finishing a book, however small.

Successful achievement in beginning reading is only the first step, however, in the ultimate process of achieving lasting interest and highly developed reading facility. There is evidence that children are not reading outside of school as widely as they should. According to Betts and Preston, schools have not been successful in liquidating functional illiteracy, or in awakening a love for reading among the majority of pupils.* If one judges reading materials on the basis of potential personality growth, one looks for readers which develop all needed reading skills, which include the many kinds of literary forms, and which provide for unique interests and abilities. Reading materials that contribute to personality development help the individual understand himself, as he is and as he is becoming. The reader becomes acquainted with the thinking of others and comes to understand the viewpoints and experience of others, if materials are designed for individual development.

Critical Questions:

Does the material extend the experience of the reader?

---

* Emmett A. Betts and Ralph C. Preston, "The Role of the Community," *Development in and through Reading, op. cit.,* p. 100.

Does the content help the learner understand himself and the world?

Does the material insure success to the child in early stages? In later stages?

How is success provided?

Are efforts made to stimulate children to read widely outside school?

PROVISION FOR INDIVIDUAL DIFFERENCES

Research in child development suggests that any group of six-year olds or seven-year olds is more different than alike. This applies to reading abilities as well as other areas of development. Although many children progress through similar patterns as they acquire reading skills, not all children are at the same stages in each ability at the same time. In gearing an instructional program to individual differences, it is necessary for teachers to plan a range of reading ability, a range which gets wider as children progress through elementary school.

Many publishers claim that individual differences are provided for in their reading series. According to one publisher, the "step-by-step" sequence of skills allows the pupil to progress at his own rate. The statement assumes that each child will be working independently and that each teacher will permit, even encourage, flexibility with regard to individual progress, but the progress will be down a single path. The lockstep large-group approach is clearly to be discouraged if the statement of the publisher is accepted. But it appears, also, that the textbook does not, in the last analysis, provide for individual variations in speed or pattern of learning; it is the teacher who must adopt teaching procedures in this regard.

Another publisher states that "because children are different and the reading process complex, no single method of reading instruction is sufficient for a well-rounded program. A combination of methods, with varying emphasis as needed, is the best system of teaching reading." Again, a publisher's statement may place the responsibility for individualizing instruction upon the teacher and limit the function of the materials themselves. There are teachers' manuals which provide suggestions for adapting materials to individual needs, the special needs of gifted students, or the corrective and remedial needs of others. Providing extensive lists of additional readings is another device for recognizing students' individual needs.

READINESS

The concept of readiness implies a "teachable moment" in the development of an individual, when he is more able to acquire a skill with ease and proficiency than he would have been previously or will be in the future. Readiness is regarded as resulting from a variety of factors; some are due to maturation and some are learned. There are text materials which include readiness activities before each new skill is presented. Such activities are viewed as a means af pacing the child rather than forcing him. However, drills and exercises do not always accomplish for a child what growth and maturation do.

In attempting to cope with the difficulties involved in developing initial reading readiness, many basic series include workbooks. Some language fluency, motor skills, recognition of shape, form, and sound may be gained from the activities of the workbook. But many authorities doubt that such workbooks actually contribute to readiness. Certainly, there are many children who have no need for a long sequence of exercises designed to develop readiness. Conversely, there are also children whose exposure to heavy doses of practice will promote negative attitudes not conducive to later reading enjoyment.

One widely prevalent plan of textbook organization is based on the assumption that readiness for reading a large number of sight words is limited during the initial stages. Under this plan, new words are introduced gradually, one new word in fifty to eighty known words. In some text materials, a further distinction is made between teaching level and independent reading level. Where this occurs, it represents an attempt to foster self-help by the learner. Where no distinction is made between teaching level and independent reading level, the format remains consistently teacher-centered with little provision for independent reading.

Another view in textbook construction assumes that children must first learn to mechanically "decode" written symbols before they can read for meaning. Heavy amounts of practice are required to master the skill of decoding, and satisfaction in reading for meaning is delayed. How ready children are for a program involving considerable drill is a question that may be raised.

Critical Questions:

Are readiness activities provided in the beginning materials and/or throughout the program to develop language fluency, motor skills, and recognition of shape, form, and sounds?

Are readiness workbooks provided?

Is help provided to the teacher in identifying and developing readiness?

Does the material differentiate between teaching level and independent reading level?

Is aid given the learner to make it possible for him to learn independently?

Are skills and facts presented and taught as prerequisite learning before reading may take place: the alphabet, phonic skills, sight words, grapheme-phoneme correspondences?

MOTIVATION AND INTEREST

Closely related to reading readiness is motivation. Many people feel that a child associates learning to read with the satisfaction of basic human wants; prime motivation for reading may develop. If a child gratifies his needs for interpersonal relationships, social approval, social acceptance, self-realization, and learning and achievement through reading, a lasting desire to read may be established. Motivation suggests a powerful force which initiates or sustains activities perceived by an individual as satisfying certain needs. Success is among the most potent of motives.

A less basic type of motivation is provided in many text materials. A variety of devices are employed. Attractive books, enjoyable stories, and amusing pictures play their part in arousing children to want to read. Using the ideas met in reading in other activities, correlating the various aspects of language into the reading program, and enrichment activities are other motivational devices that have been used widely.

The satisfaction that comes from making progress and achieving reasonable success acts as a spur to learning. Materials that lead to successful achievement are more likely to be preferred by children than materials that result in frustration.

Favorable attitudes toward reading are often brought about by "wanting to know." Materials that tell children about the world around them, satisfy curiosity, and capitalize on existing interests and concerns in and out of school have meaning for children.

Sociocultural forces affect reading motivation. Middle-class children often come to school highly motivated to read and bring with them concepts, attitudes, and values which prepare them for those they will encounter in text materials. The roles portrayed in stories are similar to those already learned at home. In lower- and working-class families the child may be denied the opportunity to develop favorable attitudes toward learning and education. He is at a further disadvantage when he encounters the people and world of the basic reader (for a more complete description of role development and the concept of self, see Chapter 3).

In the last analysis, sustained motivation occurs from the uses of materials which make possible successful achievement in the early stages of reading and which help children feel worthy and accepted. Lack of motivation occurs from the use of inappropriate materials, materials that are too easy, too difficult, or poorly paced, or whose content is unsuited to children.

Most publishers have gone to some effort and expense to provide attractive illustrations and format for text materials. At times, attractiveness has been confused with interest. This is not surprising since interest is an elusive aspect of human behavior, difficult to identify and difficult to evaluate. Interest in reading may arise from successful achievement, from some relationships of content to already existing interests, or from emphasis on topics that seem to appeal to certain age groups.

Provided that materials are so constructed that they pace each child's achievement with a suitable sequence of activities, they hold interest for children. But text materials may also capitalize upon existing interests of children and include topics that are appropriate. For example, seven-year olds already interested in pets and animals are likely to enjoy stories about cats and dogs, although plot, style, and characterization play an important part in interest (see Chapter 3).

Amusing or exciting stories are more likely to be interesting than lists of words or nonsense syllables. Varied selections which include surprise, liveliness, and humor also appeal to children. Often, materials which hold the interest of adults will have attraction for children. By the same token, materials which are dull and boring to adults may not hold children's interest, simply because they are too easy to read.

Critical Questions:

Are motivational devices and activities built into the materials?

Is help provided for the teacher to achieve general and specific motivation for learning?

Are the design, format, pictures, and other aspects sufficiently attractive to motivate interest?

Is the child's satisfaction of his needs the basis for motivation?

Does the reading material employ a variety of enrichment activities for motivation?

Do the materials create a desire to know in pupils: do they arouse curiosity, capitalize on children's interests and concerns, and provide needed knowledge about the world around them?

Does the material tap the motivational aspects of the child's own sub-culture?

Do the materials and the suggestions for use make children feel worthy and accepted?

Does the content utilize literary techniques to provide excitement, involvement, suspense, humor, and other sources of interest?

OTHER LEARNING PRINCIPLES

Historically, there have been two concepts of man as a learner. The first regards man as possessing a mind and faculties, such as reasoning, remembering, and imagining. These faculties grow with exercise; therefore, practice and drill are important and motivation and individual differences are irrelevant. According to this theory, what is learned in one situation is automatically transferred to all other situations.

The second concept regards man as an energy system attempting to maintain equilibrium. This concept includes two different ideas about learning:

(a) The behaviorist theories which attempt to establish responses to specific stimuli. Practice or drill is essential. Motivation is controlled from without by conditioning, rewards, or responses.

(b) The Gestalt or field theories which assume that cognitive processes are fundamental. Responses are shaped by purpose. Learning is essentially an active process of selecting and organizing or giving meaning to what is perceived.*

Text materials which introduce lists of words in isolation lean heavily on faculty psychology. Word identification is presumed to occur separately from considerations of word meaning or context. Since transfer is assumed to be automatic, the writers of such materials believe that no problem exists when children advance from identifying words in isolation to reading meaningful sentences, paragraphs, and stories. Because motivation and individual differences are not involved in faculty psychology, there is little need for involving pupil purposes, frames of reference, or social processes in planning for learning.

The behaviorist theories of learning support materials which provide immediate reward or reinforcement for correct responses to certain stimuli. Concepts and habits are learned through association and practice. The materials

---

* Hilda Taba, *Curriculum Development Theory and Practice* (New York: Harcourt, Brace & World, Inc., 1962), pp. 79–81.

contain frequent opportunities for responding to situations; the more the response is used, the stronger the association. Purpose, thought, and insight in learning are subordinate to the reinforcement of correct responses. Various programs for learning and teaching machines are based upon behaviorist theories.

The critics of behaviorism as a learning theory point out that there are other forces operating, determined by the nature and complexity of the stimulus and the disposition of the learner. Also, the theory does not provide for understanding, thinking, or reconstructing. The stress on habit formation, or "operant conditioning," as B. F. Skinner terms his method of shaping behavior, leads to a lack of emphasis upon the active role of the learner.

The Gestalt or field theorists are responsible for introducing complex concepts of learning and problem solving. According to these theories, learning involves more than remembering. Learning is, therefore, not a mechanical response stamped into a habit, but a form of intelligent behavior that takes place when a problem is presented. The learner, in searching for a solution to the problem confronting him, may perceive the total field in which he encounters new experiences or may perceive those parts that will help him solve the problem. The learning process is conceived of as the resolving of tensions, existing because a problem was introduced. The perceptual field is reorganized as the learner searches for a solution to the problem. Insight or sudden solution is followed by closure.

The critics of cognitive learning argue that the criteria of insightful learning do not differentiate enough from trial and error; that inner reorganization is assumed makes Gestalt theory difficult to test experimentally.

Materials which derive from Gestalt or field theory usually provide for the introduction of ideas in familiar context. The context or field setting aids in learning new words and appears to be superior as an initial step in learning written language. The use of complete units of meaning in reading materials makes possible identification of unknown words through the process of thought or insight. Reading is purposeful, undertaken to solve existing problems or attain desired goals which makes for learning efficiency. According to this view, unthinking repetitive drill is to be avoided, as is the application of rules taught by rote.

Actually, according to various educational psychologists, none of the existing behaviorist or Gestalt theories yet yields a comprehensive view of learning, sufficiently general to guide all aspects of classroom practice. Instead, the teacher with a knowledge of learning principles derived from many theories can base practice upon those which appear to promote effective learning. Although there is disagreement as to what actually happens within the learner, there are those principles of learning which complement each other in their emphases. Examples of such principles are included in the following questions.

Critical Questions:

Is a theory of learning stated or implied in the material? What is it?

Is the material consistent with a stated or implied theory of learning?

Is the teacher helped to understand and apply the theory of learning?

Does the material prepare the child for learning by arousing interest, helping him acquire a mental set for learning, presenting him with a background adequate for the new learning, and preparing him to take action or respond in some way?

Does the material create "an appropriate" or "manageable level of anxiety" or curiosity within the child so that his attention is focused on the stimulus or problem to be solved?

Is the material presented in such a way as to provide the learner with auditory as well as visual stimuli? Can the child learn to bring to the printed word the same response pattern he has previously brought to the spoken word?

Does the material permit the child to draw on his fund of meaning so that he can integrate new meanings with the old?

Does the material permit the child to systematize or organize his knowledge or to acquire insight?

Does the material permit the child to use his learning actively in new situations or to generalize his learnings?

Does the material permit the child to complete a task and avoid the confusion of inadequate learning?

Does the material provide distributed practice rather than massed practices in the learning of skills and abilities?

SUMMARY

Materials designed for teaching reading have been influenced by the principles of child development and learning theory. Because learning to read is a complex process requiring a relatively long time, levels of reading achievement can be identified which are closely related to similar stages in the growth and development of children. These stages of development are reflected in materials adapted to the physical, emotional, and social characteristics of growing boys and girls, and to differences in learning readiness.

Although at present a precise and unified theory is lacking, the learning process can be described by certain principles upon which there is general agreement. These include the recognition of individual differences in ability and rate of learning, the importance of motivation in facilitating learning, and the superiority of meaningful materials and tasks.

Chapter 3

Sociocultural

Principles

The importance of social influences upon people has long been the subject of investigation by sociologists and anthropologists. Social forces affect values, attitudes, beliefs, behavior patterns, understandings, interests, and needs. The social environment a child is reared in and the behavior patterns shaped by it are significant in determining his self-concept and his attitudes toward the world.

Attitudes, values, interests, role expectancies and how to play these roles, and the acquisition of self-concept are achieved through the child's associations with others in a variety of groups and social institutions. Teachers have long been aware that the attitudes of a pupil are directed toward the school and the tasks he is expected to do. Attitudes toward learning to read and what he wishes to read about are shaped through the child's experiences.

A child's background of experience shapes his dispositions to behave and defines the limits of his expectations in given situations. The social environment of a child assists him in establishing the behavior patterns expected of him. The child becomes aware of codes of behavior and of conflicts among these codes. His social environment equips him with characteristic modes of responding to given stimuli. These modes of responding include language patterns the child learns to use when he needs to communicate. He learns the particular language patterns of the primary group, which is nearly always the family.

Language patterns are learned largely through imitation and emulation. They are learned because they are usually the most significant model of language available to the child. The child's specific set of language patterns is unique for him and is referred to as his ideolect, which falls within his sub-culture's dialect.

Each child comes to school with his own language. His language may or may not correspond to the language of the teacher, the text, or other pupils. Language is a result of social influences; and language influences are not everywhere the same.

An examination of five sociocultural factors serves as a framework for identifying and discussing principles that may be of value in analyzing reading texts and materials: interest, social class and experience, dialect differences, role development, and values.

WHAT CHILDREN LIKE TO READ

The importance of interest as a factor in learning to read has been stressed for many years. Interest is thought by many to be more critical in learning than intelligence. Teachers often remark that if only they could get the children interested, they would learn to read.

What are the reading interests of boys and girls? About three hundred studies of reading interests have been reported and the findings of these studies are in striking agreement. These are among the more significant conclusions:

1. In the early grades, boys and girls have similar interests in reading. Young children prefer stories dealing with familiar experiences. They enjoy stories about pets, toys, children, real and imaginary animals, fairy tales,

nature stories that are fanciful, and humorous stories that are direct and which relate to personal experiences.

2. Children in the primary grades are interested in a greater variety of reading materials than are older children, but show less discrimination in their selection of materials. Interests change gradually and become more sharply differentiated about the time children move into the fourth grade.

3. Distinct differences in reading interests are noticeable beginning in the middle grades. Children in these grades indicate a preference for action, adventure, surprise, and humor. Great interest in comics begins in the middle grades and continues into junior high school. Middle grade children enjoy realistic animal stories, stories of children in other lands, myths, legends, and hero and folk tales. As children progress through the grades, they exhibit a marked increase in interest in mystery stories, while interest in cowboy stories and fairy tales decreases. Interest in Westerns reaches its peak in the fifth grade and then declines rapidly. Interest in art and music declines after grade five. Interest in sports increases slowly reaching a peak in high school. Interest in science is relatively new and increases gradually through the ninth grade, but does not become as popular as adventure, mystery, and sports.

4. Interests are affected by age, sex, intelligence, and socioeconomic status. Increasing maturity affects the selection of reading materials. The number of fields reported as areas of interest decreases with age; individual responses indicate a narrower range with increasing age. But there remains a wide range of differences among pupils of a given age, particularly in junior high school. The amount of voluntary reading increases through eighth grade and then noticeably decreases through high school.

There are more significant differences in reading interests between boys and girls than between groups of children from dissimilar socioeconomic areas. Beginning about age eight, preferences for reading materials are modified on the basis of sex. Middle grade boys tend to reject stories about girls or about girlish topics, though girls often choose books dealing with boys or which appeal to boys, particularly adventure stories, and girls read more than boys do.

Bright pupils read more and the stories are of higher quality. They prefer factual materials. Pupils of average and below average intelligence have similar reading interests. Those below average intelligence particularly prefer stories dealing with familiar experiences.

5. Elementary school pupils read more fiction than other kinds of materials. They prefer prose to poetry; girls find poetry more satisfying than boys do. Books chosen by boys are characterized by strong plots and dominant male characters. Boys' selections include stories about animals, adventure, patriotism, games, sports, out-of-doors exploration, hobbies, and handicrafts. Boys also indicate preferences for science, history, travel, biographies of men, and war. Adult magazines are popular with both boys and girls, but children's magazines are not usually popular with boys.

A number of reading interests indicated by middle grade girls are similar to those of boys. Girls enjoy adventure stories, patriotism, animals, humor, and mystery. Distinct differences due to sex are noted in girls' choices of stories of love and romance, sentiment, home and family life, women's activities, and biographies of great women. Girls prefer poetry more than do boys and their interest is for stories of love and romance; however, these were second to humor and comedy for all ages.

Probably the most striking factor about reading interests is the tremendous range of individual differences. While general knowledge of reading interests is quite useful to the teacher, it is widely agreed that the teacher must determine the needs and interests of each child. Within a group of children of similar age, background of experience, and intelligence, there exists a wide range of reading interests. Intensive study of each child is necessary if he is to be introduced to the right book at the right time, to take advantage of existing interests or develop new ones.

While there is considerable evidence that adults are able to select books that children find interesting, evidence is also available that in many cases adults are not tuned in to the reading interests of children.

Many selections commonly used in reading programs are better liked by girls than boys. This suggests that much more attention should be given to the selection of materials which will interest boys. This becomes even more important since boys constitute by far the larger percentage of reading disability cases. Reading authorities agree that there is considerable likelihood that including many more stories interesting to boys contributes to greater success in reading and results in far fewer cases of reading disability. The interests of pupils should be considered when reading materials are selected. Two questions may be important in this consideration. First, do the materials reflect the known reading interests of pupils of the age and sex for whom they were prepared? Knowledge of reading interests assists in analyzing the extent to which materials are in harmony with the expressed interests of a particular sex and age group. Second, do the materials extend and develop a rich variety of reading interests? To what extent do the materials help stimulate pupils to broaden their interests? Reading materials can help pupils enrich their background of reading interests and develop appreciation for a variety of topics and materials. Experience indicates that the pupil who is willing to read only about the Civil War or to read only horse stories can be stimulated to extend his reading horizons through the use of appropriate reading materials. These two questions are not contradictory; they are mutually supportive. Those who believe that children's interests are very important in the elementary school reading program will wish to furnish boys and girls with materials that extend and enrich interests as well as enhance existing ones.

Critical Questions:

To what extent do the materials reflect the reading interests of children of the age and sex and background they were designed for?

Do the materials extend and develop a rich variety of reading interests? If so, how?

Are provisions made for meeting the interests of both boys and girls? In what way is this done?

How are differences in interests related to intelligence and socioeconomic background provided for?

SOCIAL CLASS AND EXPERIENCE

Sociologists and anthropologists have accumulated a great deal of evidence that class structure is a primary source of the influences which affect people's lives. The effects of social class are seen in occupational choices, recreation, place of residence, purchasing habits, government, and education. However, the social experiences of Americans vary widely. This accounts for the great range of differences in behavior, interests, expectations, values, and attitudes.

The associations an individual has as a member of a social class are important means by which he learns. The predominant values and attitudes of a given social class are transmitted to the child through formal and informal learning by the parents.

As the child extends his associations beyond the family into the community, what has been learned in the home is reinforced, modified, and expanded. Social experiences thus establish attitudes, values, and interests; determine the nature of expectations and the character of drive exhibited in pursuit of goals; and define the limits of expected behavior. They prescribe the roles an individual must play and how he is to play them. Membership in a particular social class assigns a status position to the individual, and contributes to the development of his self-concept.

While Americans reject the notion of different social levels, research has clearly demonstrated that social class structure exists and is a potent influence in the development of the individual. Acquaintance with the characteristics of social class structure contributes to an understanding of the beliefs, attitudes, and interests of children who have been reared in different classes. The wide range of characteristics of the various social classes has significance for teachers, supervisors, and administrators as they analyze and select reading materials.

Three social class levels are generally recognized, as evidenced by the popular usage of "upper," "middle," and "lower" class. Sociologists, such as Warner and Hollingshead, have identified five or six distinct levels depending on geographic location and age of community. However, this section will briefly describe the characteristics of only three classes. The reader is cautioned not to apply these generalizations too liberally to the group he teaches. These descriptions are given as illustrations of the diversity of background among groups of children.

The first group occupies the highest social level and

constitutes a small percentage of the total population—usually about 12 percent. Members of this group consider education to be particularly important in preserving the status quo. Nearly every child attends college, but these must be the "right" schools. Parents are greatly concerned that their children achieve success, and they view education as being essential to success. However, they seldom take an active interest in the school affairs below the college level. The nation's readers are found in this group. They tend to read conservative newspapers, and are interested in national and international news and financial affairs. They read a wide range of magazines, such as *Harper's* and the *Atlantic Monthly*. Their interests in books lean toward the classics, novels, history, and biography. Though they provide a variety of books for their children and otherwise make contact with books a possibility, in many cases they exert little influence on their reading interests. This is probably true because parents spend relatively little time with children during their early years.

The members of group two constitute the largest group. Preoccupation with making a living and running the home keeps the parents from exercising rigid control over the children. The children are permitted considerable freedom, and, therefore, their social experiences are largely gained from contacts at neighborhood playgrounds and in organizations such as the Scouts and the Little League. Their experiences and interests are different from those of children in group one. They are more liberal than children in group one and have less well-defined objectives for their lifework. They are taught that they will be responsible for their future success, and that whatever they become will be the result of their own effort.

While they respect education highly, only about one half of the children take college preparatory courses in high school. Those who want their children to go to college work hard to make it possible. This group also has a wide variety of reading interests; they read the more popular magazines and prefer the more liberal newspapers. They hold books in high regard but read them only occasionally. Many provide books for their children and encourage them to use the library.

Group three constitutes the last group in the social structure. The majority of its members are referred to as "honest, but poor," but it includes those who are often thought of as having a bad reputation and as being lazy and having no aspiration. Many members of group three are not convinced of the value of an education and large numbers have not finished high school. Most of them want their children to go to high school, but little protest is made if they drop out. Children grow up not expecting to attend college. Very little time is spent in reading and it is not encouraged by the parents. Movies, televiewing, and conversing with neighbors are favorite pastimes.

The children are permitted considerable freedom, and consequently spend much time away from home and the direct influence of the parents. They play in the street, vacant lots, and neighborhood parks. They have limited contact with parents in such activities as hobbies and similar recreations. Their associations in neighborhood cliques and gangs often results in the acquisition of interests and attitudes that oppose those of the school. Their background of experiences has limited their range of expectations.

The reading habits of group three run to newspapers which play up crime and sensational stories and to magazines of low literary quality. Books are rarely read and very few are found in the home. Those read are usually detective stories and stories involving romance and adventure; very few best-selling books find their way into these homes. The lack of interest in reading by the parents is reflected in the reading habits of the children. Children are not encouraged to read and little use is made of library facilities by either adults or children.

This brief description of social class structure points out the disparity in behavior, interests, and attitudes among Americans. Backgrounds of experience vary greatly from one social class to another, and the expectations and aspirations of the various groups are significantly different. Knowledge of social class characteristics makes it possible for teachers to anticipate the range of experiences of children, and to predict the attitudes and interests of individual pupils.

Those who face the task of selecting appropriate reading materials must take the children's background of experiences into consideration. Knowing the social class membership of children enables analysts to search out reading materials likely to fit their experiences and interests. Children develop reading skills as they relate story content to their own experiences. Familiar situations depicted in stories help the child to extend his understanding of story content. Familiar content reinforces past learning by substantiating what has been learned. Story content that is familiar to children may help them develop more mature concepts. Children are more easily motivated by a story which they can relate to their own experiences.

Knowledge of social class background assists selectors in providing a variety of reading materials appealing to pupils of disparate backgrounds. A child from the upper class is more likely to have traveled, had music lessons, and attended concerts, museums, and the theater than is a child from the lower class. Language development is more highly advanced in children from the upper class. These factors contribute to the development of interests and tastes, unlike those children from other social classes. Children from the lower class usually have received little encouragement to read and have not been exposed to reading materials of high literary quality. Reading is not valued very highly among these children and, therefore, relatively few of them have built up positive attitudes toward it. If the teacher is to develop within children a desire to read, then the materials used play a fundamental role.

Teachers need to know more than the social class membership of children; knowledge of the experiential background of every child is very important. When children are members of the same social class, there are many common elements in their backgrounds of experience. However, the sum of the experiences each one brings to school with him is unique. No two children have exactly the same social experiences. There is relatively wide latitude within each social class; the class limits are not sharply drawn.

Not only are there many possibilities for deviation within one social class, but most children have experiences with members of other social classes. These contacts may be fleeting or they may be relatively permanent. In any event, these experiences across class lines help blur class limits and provide a broader background of experience than would otherwise be possible. Knowledge of differences in the experiential background of groups of children may be vital in searching out appropriate materials for the instructional reading program. The readiness for specific instructional techniques to a large extent depends upon the experiences of children prior to implementation of those techniques.

Knowledge of experience of individual pupils enables the teacher to select reading materials which may extend the experience of the children. Knowing, for example, that a pupil has some understanding of space travel, the teacher helps the child broaden his knowledge by providing books on related topics. Reading becomes in itself a part of a child's experiential background and enables him to share vicariously in a variety of experiences. The child expands his horizons because he is able to share the experiences of the past, present, and future.

Critical Questions:

Is the content of the reading materials appropriate to the social class background of the children who use them? Does it make sense to them? Is content an important aspect of the program espoused by the authors of the materials? Is the content familiar to the children? Are they likely to relate it to what they have experienced?

To what extent do the materials promote a desire to read? How is this handled?

Are social classes characterized accurately?

Are story settings common ones for the readers?

How do the materials help prepare children for new learning yet to come? Are there provisions for developing readiness?

How do the materials contribute to expanding the experiential background of children?

DIALECT DIFFERENCES

By the time children enter school they have become quite competent users of language. All children in the United States do not learn exactly the same language because they are reared in divergent cultural, socioeconomic, and regional groups. Language patterns tend to vary among these groups. Many dialects are spoken in a metropolitan area; the language spoken in the schools mirrors the speech patterns of the community.

Perhaps the most noticeable differences are regional. Differences in dialect frequently help to distinguish one speaker from another. A variety of regional dialects are heard in most metropolitan areas, as well as on television and radio.

The specific groups in which children find primary associations set the standards for acceptable language patterns. The processes by which these standards are set are usually informal and difficult to identify, although the child who does not use the dominant language pattern is sometimes made painfully aware of his divergence. Teenagers are well known for their caustic remarks directed at the person who is not up-to-date in the use of currently popular slang. Differences in dialect are apparent in the pronunciation of words, the use of idiomatic expressions, and the use of slang expressions.

Probably the most recognizable difference in dialect is in the pronunciation of particular words. The proper pronunciation of *ration, hog, coupon, Caribbean,* and *schedule* is much debated. Yet it is fairly evident that correctness in such cases is a matter of where one was reared.

Words are not pronounced the same by all groups of people and the criterion of communication usually does not demand this. A Michigan third-grader described his knowledge of the letters a, e, i, o, u and informed his parents that these were the "valz." It became clear upon investigation that his teacher was raised in a Southern state, but this did not stand in the way of his learning about vowels. A man from Ohio will characteristically sound the "tt" in Betty as "dd," while a man from Colorado will sound it as "tt." Some groups of people give "g" in words ending in "ing" the sound of "g" in gun, while others do not pronounce it at all. A man in Brooklyn may tell about the "boid" he saw, while a Chicagoan may refer to "dat" bird. Dialects characteristic of those who learned English as a second language have long been standard comedy fare in this country. These dialects, while perhaps overdrawn, are readily identifiable. These prounuciations are indicative of speech patterns learned by individuals as members of particular groups. However, communication rarely is seriously impeded by differences in pronunciation.

The use of idiomatic expressions unique to a regional area or subcultural group is another important dialect difference. Idioms are learned as a part of the language and become communication units for the user. Large numbers of idioms are shared by members of special groups, and in many cases the outsider attaches little or no meaning to them since comprehension of each idiom is dependent upon intimate knowledge of the culture of the group. This is particularly noticeable in metropolitan areas where many people with the same ethnic background tend to segregate themselves and live as a group and where other groups are segregated on the basis of social, economic, racial, or religious factors.

The children in a particular group learn to use the language of their parents modified by the language of the community. They learn to use the idiomatic expressions peculiar to their group. For example, it may surprise the outsider to learn that within certain groups a person goes "down below" when he travels south, and that he will walk along a river when invited to "walk the branch."

Slang expressions are used by nearly everyone. These become a second language for some groups and become *the* language for some teenagers. While the use of slang, particularly among teenagers, seems to be universal, the items of slang expression are not the same from group to group. Slang is, perhaps, the cutting edge of language. It is constantly changing. What is up-to-date one day may be passé and inappropriate the next. Neither is slang everywhere the same. It differs from one locality or region to another, and among social and vocational groups.

Some who have studied the problems that complicate teaching reading believe that children would achieve better if they learned to read using materials which reflected their particular dialect. A person's dialect is his means of communication. Teachers often expect pupils to pronounce words "correctly," speak in "complete sentences" and not use "ain't," "he done it," and "set down." The children in these situations are being asked to change their language pattern because it is not acceptable to the teacher. In many cases, what this means is that children must not only cope with reading instruction but they must do it while learning what, to them, is essentially a foreign language. This is quite a lot to expect of elementary school children.

Dialect is closely interwoven with the culture. It is the means by which the culture expresses itself as the members engage in communication. To reject a particular dialect is to reject the culture. Such rejection is usually accompanied by conflict of varying degree. Children are most often those who encounter and, therefore, must resolve such conflicts.

Despite the problems raised for many children, most teachers apparently believe that all children should be introduced to the dominant language pattern at the beginning of their school experience. There is abundant evidence that many children can surmount the difficulties this imposes. There is much evidence that while many dialects continue to exist, a dominant pattern of language has emerged in the United States. Television, radio, movies, and other mass communication media have assisted this development. A great many school patrons join with practitioners in believing that children who fail to learn the dominant language pattern are seriously handicapped in later life.

Critical Questions:

Is there a recognition of and provision for dialect differences in the materials? If so, how is it handled? Will some children be unduly penalized by the language patterns used?

Are the materials designed for one dialect group or for all children? If the former, is the dialect presented accurately?

In materials based on phonic or linguistic principles, are differences in pronunciation possible and acceptable?

Are the idioms included in the materials appropriate to the level of understanding and dialect of the children who will use them?

Is slang used in the materials? If so, is it up-to-date, appropriate, and meaningful to the children who will use the materials?

Do the materials introduce the dominant language pattern consistently and accurately?

Are words and phrases with special meaning or double entendre in some dialects handled carefully?

ROLE DEVELOPMENT

An essential characteristic of social growth is the development of the roles a person is expected to learn. The particular social forces and dynamics existing at a given point in the culture define the limits of acceptable behavior of various members of the culture. Behavior which is appropriate for a five-year-old boy is no longer appropriate at age eight and would cause grave doubts about an adult male who engaged in it. Girls of high school age are expected to act differently from grandmothers; automobile mechanics do not behave in the same way as salesladies in a department store. These differences in behavior are due to differences in role expectations held by members of society. Individuals learn those behavior patterns associated with given roles.

Learning the roles appropriate to the variety of situations

he finds himself in is an essential aspect of the social growth of an individual. As the child grows older and has more experiences, he learns a larger variety of roles. At times the child is made painfully aware that playground behavior is unacceptable in the classroom. Applause which may be appropriate at the movies is found to be quite out of place during religious services. Certain behavior patterns are found to elicit approval in one situation and rejection in another. Reprimands for behavior defined as inappropriate in one situation may be replaced by compliments and praise for the same behavior in another situation.

Feedback received in his association with others assists the individual to learn the roles expected of him in various situations. Each person learns a variety of roles and adjusts his behavior according to the expectations defined by society.

Role development is seen by many educators as important in reading materials. The materials may present a variety of situations and models from which pupils learn appropriate behavior. Those who take this position believe that identification with story characters as "significant others" contributes to an assessment of the range and variety of roles which exist, and contributes to the development of roles appropriate to given situations. Boys learn how boys behave and how men behave. Girls learn how girls behave and how women behave. Each learns that it is usually inappropriate to behave in ways associated with the opposite sex.

Reading materials contribute to the development of roles appropriate to boys and girls and to men and women by presenting situations in which appropriate behavior is associated with or ascribed to given models. Story characters can be portrayed in roles which reflect those found acceptable in the culture. Characters of various ages, engaged in pursuits and behaving in ways usually associated with a particular age and sex, may provide models for readers and assist them in knowing the variety of roles open to them and to the groups they belong to. They learn the limits of behavior associated with each role. At the same time readers may learn which behavior patterns are unacceptable in a given role.

There is a considerable body of opinion that reading contributes to role development. As pupils identify with story characters, they gain insight into the range and variety of behavior and into the factors which motivate behavior. Reading helps children become aware of acceptable patterns of behavior and adjust their behavior to meet the demands of a variety of situations. The reader who sees himself in the role of a story character may assume a similar role because of strong identification. On the other hand, he may assume a different role in an attempt to project himself as an individual. Children learn to gauge their behavior in terms of norms expressed in reading. Through reading, children encounter experiences and problems similar to their own, and as a result increase their ability to solve their problems and mature in self-understanding. Reading offers the possibility of widening horizons and deepening insights into the tremendous range of human behavior, and aids in understanding behavior required in specific situations. Reading enables children to learn new roles and to modify existing ones.

In analyzing reading materials for their contribution to role development, seven questions may assist us:

1. Are the activities engaged in by various story characters appropriate to the roles usually ascribed to them in the general culture?

   Children reinforce their concepts about appropriate behavior by recognizing through reading materials that others, like themselves, are usually found playing certain games, enjoying certain hobbies, and engaging in certain household chores. Play and recreational activity depicted in reading materials call for some roles to be assumed by boys and others by girls.

Young readers mature their understanding of roles appropriate to adults by the activities engaged in by adult characters. The work and recreational activities engaged in strengthen the recognition that such pursuits are masculine or feminine in character. The household responsibilities assigned to story characters contribute to the reader's knowledge of adult roles.

2. Are appropriate models for behavior available in the materials?

The nature and kinds of models available are important in influencing role development. Children emulate the behavior of those whom they see as occupying prestige or important positions or who play important roles. The pressure in the culture of folk heroes, mythological characters, and current idols (both imaginary and real) is evidence that people take cues for behavior from models thought to represent those values and attitudes worth emulating. Fads in dress, habits, and behavior are evidence that we tend to imitate models.

Characters, both imaginary and real, exist in all societies as significant others for the members of that society. The concept of the significant other was proposed by George Mead to assist in understanding human behavior. Young children modify their behavior to correspond with their conception of a culture hero, such as Daniel Boone or Abraham Lincoln, or of an imaginary character such as Uncle Sam or Pecos Bill.

3. With whom do the story characters associate?

Insight into the nature of social relationships may be gained by reading. Through the choice of playmates, friends, neighbors, and partners, reading mate rials expand knowledge about the many ways people build associations with one another. Reading about many kinds of associations contributes to an understanding of acceptable behavior. It also assists in making appropriate choices from among alternatives. Reading materials present a broad range of situations involving intimate social relationships which help individuals become sensitive to the problems, needs, customs, and interests of others. They find through wide reading that social situations require flexibility in feeling and acting. They learn to adjust behavior according to the requirements of different situations. They discover what is expected of them as they engage in the give-and-take of the social world. They grow toward maturity as they learn to cope with the demands of divergent social situations.

4. What is the constituency of the family group?

The structure of the family as depicted in reading materials influences the development of role. The usual family in reading texts is composed of father, mother, sister, brother and baby. Baby is usually a girl. A variety of family structures may assist the reader to refine his conception of the role of various family members. Relationships among family members contribute to an understanding of how the individual is expected to act. Families which include one or more grandparents, or an aunt or an uncle, have different expectations for the individuals in the family. Relationships which children establish with their grandparents differ from those with parents or with siblings. Stepmothers, stepfathers, half-sisters and half-brothers may affect the family structure so that behavioral expectations are altered. The absence of one or both parents affects role development.

Not all reading materials contribute to an understanding of the effects of various family structures since many materials do not involve family groups or do so indirectly. Even in those materials which do involve the family the analyst must recognize that patterns of behavior for a given individual may vary considerably from one family structure to another. The oldest boy in a family having no father assumes a different role than the oldest boy whose father lives with the family.

5. Is the story setting predominantly urban, rural, or suburban?

While there are striking similarities among those living in various settings, there are equally striking differences in their roles. Many household tasks that urban family members accept differ significantly from those of suburban and rural families. The suburban family often builds different relationships with its neighbors than does the city or farm family. Reading materials which include many social settings enable readers to escape from building stereotypes about the behavior a child or adult should exhibit. Behavior patterns can differ and still be acceptable.

6. What occupations are represented, and how?

Acquaintance with a range of occupations can assist readers in knowing which patterns of behavior are associated with given occupations. Occupations can be presented in a positive or negative way and thus contribute not only to an understanding of the occupational role, but also to patterns of acceptance or rejection of these occupations.

Occupations may be presented in ways that suggest they are menial and that those who do such work are unworthy, unskilled, and incapable or lack the desire to do work which carries more prestige. At the ideal level, collecting garbage is socially useful and important work. Yet at the real level, such work does not carry prestige and is not seen as desirable. Much criticism has been directed at many current reading texts because the father is pictured as a white-collar worker who carries a briefcase and commutes to work.

It is rather frequently stated that this presents a restricted and unrealistic picture of vocations in the
United States. Recently, new materials that picture
blue collar workers have appeared.

7. How are story characters dressed?

It has been said that those who are slovenly in dress
are slovenly in behavior, and that those who dress
neatly exhibit behavior to match. While this is only
a cliché, there is ample evidence that clothing, as well
as behavior, is associated with given roles. Knowledge
of appropriate behavior, therefore, may be gained by
giving attention to the manner in which people dress.

Reading materials can provide excellent opportunities for readers to become acquainted with many customs and habits of dress. Illustrations as well as text
contribute to the development of concepts about the
clothing worn by persons occupying different roles.
Accurate portrayal of customs of dress and hair styles
assist the reader in knowing what dress is appropriate
in a range of situations.

Critical Questions:

Are the activities engaged in by story characters appropriate to the roles usually ascribed to them in the general
culture?

Are appropriate models for behavior in the materials?

With whom do the story characters associate?

What is the constituency of the family group? What is
the pattern of relationships within the family?

Is the story setting predominantly urban, rural, or suburban? Are the roles pictured realistically and accurately
in these settings?

What occupations are shown and how are they represented? Are a variety included? Are hidden value judgments a part of the presentation?

How are story characters dressed?

VALUES

The development of values is inseparably linked to the total growth of the individual. One is almost forced to consider values in discussing interests, beliefs, attitudes, or behavior. The development of roles is directly related to the development of values. The roles an individual learns to play not only modify his values but also are the channels through which he expresses them.

Values develop as the individual interacts with his environment. The variety of experiences engaged in shapes and molds his value structure. However, the quality of experience is more important than quantity.

Children's values are developed in a variety of ways; it is generally assumed that one of the most important is wide reading. That values exist in reading materials is a matter of record. They are found in story characters and situations. Descriptive passages are often heavily value-laden. And in poetry and certain prose selections, values are found in the mood created by cadence, rhythm, and movement.

There is conflicting opinion and evidence, however, of the effects of reading on children's values. While the majority of reading authorities believe that values are affected by reading, there is little research evidence to substantiate or refute this. There are also some experts who are convinced that content is not important in *learning* the basic reading skills. Therefore, the possible effects of reading on values need not be consideration in the selection of reading materials for the early grades. It should be stressed that this pertains only to materials used in skill development and not those used in other stages of the reading program.

The content of reading materials in America has reflected the importance generally attached to the development of values through reading. From the New England Primer to the McGuffy Readers to present-day basal readers, the predominant values of the day have found expression.

The importance of democratic ideals is apparent in the variety of reading materials depicting situations in which cooperation, fair play, liberty, justice, and equality are portrayed as not only desirable but essential. Reading materials rich in democratic ideals are believed to contribute to the development of these values.

Value-laden reading materials are also used to foster an awareness that values may be either negative or positive. Those who take this position believe that reading assists children in translating their values into socially acceptable patterns of behavior, that reading materials which portray values in a positive manner contribute to social understanding and foster wholesome attitudes toward the self and toward others.

Moral and spiritual values, such as courage, perseverance, trust, honesty, integrity, and courtesy, are generally recognized as important and are stressed in reading materials. They are included for their possible contributions to character building and to self-confidence.

Increased tolerance is thought to develop through reading about the habits, customs, and values of others. This is particularly true in developing greater understanding of racial and religious minority groups. Myths concerning individuals, groups, and institutions may be dispelled. Superstition may be reduced. Personal prejudice may be opened to analysis. Increased understanding of the problems of others leads to sympathy and may reduce prejudices. Religious values in reading materials are believed to have a positive effect upon children by bringing increased religiosity and enhancement of the dignity and worth of the individual.

Taste, appreciation, and sensitivity are probably affected

by the aesthetic and spiritual values of reading materials. Poetry may be particularly effective in enriching children's experiences and in stimulating perceptions about "truth and beauty." Materials which promote appreciation for these values may foster humility without sacrificing self-assurance.

On the other hand, there are opposing views on the effects of reading on children's values. There is some evidence that the effects of reading on values are limited in two ways: negative values as well as positive values may develop, or there may be no discernible change in values.

Children may not accept the ideals they encounter in reading materials. Because of past experiences, they may reject those values or attach little significance to them. Experiences with reading materials which express generally accepted values in a positive manner may confirm for the child his belief that cooperation and sharing are signs of weakness. This is not necessarily the fault of the materials; they may have been misused or inappropriate for that child.

There is no assurance that reading about a family situation in which affection, love, and loyalty are portrayed will result in the development of these values. Children may reject books in which there are problems thought to be similar to those they encounter. This may be because they cannot accept the way the problem was handled in the book, or because they see no connection between the story problems and their own. Story situations involving certain moral and spiritual values may repel the young reader rather than attract him. The hero may be too good to be true or he may be sissified.

Reading may confirm a child's suspicion that winning is the important thing or that crime *does* pay. It may convince a child that his most important goal in life is to take care of himself even at the expense of others. As a result of reading, children may be persuaded to eschew values that are cherished by the majority or the dominant group.

While the thought of promoting negative values causes great concern, there are a number of reasons why this is possible. Not all groups in society accept the values held by the majority in this country. The positive effects of reading may be restricted by the tendency of people, including children, to select materials which complement existing interests, attitudes, and values. Biases remain unchanged or are strengthened, stereotypes persist, and prejudices go unchallenged.

Reading is recognized by many as being effective in reinforcing and modifying attitudes and values already partially developed within the individual. Reading by itself probably does little to stimulate appreciation for values. It stands little chance of triggering a fundamental reorganization of a child's value structure. All of a child's experiences together create within him the predisposition for change.

Critical Questions:

What values are intentionally presented? Are the values of the general culture reflected in the reading materials?

Are the values expressed portrayed in a positive manner? If so, do they tend to stimulate appreciation and acceptance?

Are negative values expressed in such a manner as to encourage rejection? Would the material incidentally develop undesirable values?

Do the values expressed complement the known values of the group the materials are intended for? Do characters act in ways which fit a desirable value structure? Are values presented with too heavy a hand? Do the materials preach too much? Is assistance given to the teacher in identifying values presented and following up on these values?

SUMMARY

Among the important criteria to be considerd in selecting textbooks, workbooks, and similar instructional materials are those of a sociological origin. Five sociocultural factors serve as a framework for identifying principles that may be of value in analyzing reading texts and other reading materials: interest, social class and experience, dialect differences, role development, and values.

Chapter 4

Educational

Principles

Educational principles have been developed through research, experience, and logic related directly to classroom use. These principles have not been developed in a vacuum; they result from study of everyday teaching situations. They draw from psychological, sociocultural, linguistic, and literary knowledge for additional meaning.

Educational principles are perhaps those most commonly included among criteria for analyzing reading materials. Educators tend to accept them as the foundation for any examination of elementary school instructional reading programs. Despite this, there are many educational principles frequently ignored or unknown by analysts, and other principles that may be quite inappropriate in some situations. The presentation and discussion of principles that follow may assist educators in effectively analyzing reading materials.

SEQUENCE, SCOPE, AND INTEGRATION

All curricular materials that attempt to build competencies must provide for sequence, scope, and integration.

In analyzing reading materials for sequence, scope, and integration, four questions may be useful.*

---

* David H. Russell, *Children Learn to Read,* 2nd ed. (Boston: Ginn and Company, 1961), pp. 148–49. Russell presents these four principles as those most important in constructing modern basic reading series.

1. Do they provide continuity of growth in reading skills, habits, and attitudes? Materials for beginning readers usually gradually introduce new words, longer lines, longer paragraphs, unfamiliar concepts, and complex sentences. The goal is to provide materials through which children can advance with relatively little guidance from the teacher. In upper grades, the reading materials provided usually give pupils experiences in locating materials on particular pages, gaining the sequence of ideas in a selection, interpreting paragraphs, practicing the skills of word recognition in context, and independently reading materials with controlled vocabularies.

2. Do they provide for a wide variety of reading activities? Two general types of activities are usually included: skill-developing activities and informal or recreational reading activities. Two illustrations of skill-developing activities are: skimming for one or two specific facts and finding answers to specific questions; informal or recreational type activities focus on reading for enjoyment.

3. Do they provide a complete organization of reading experiences? Most reading materials are constructed to avoid gaps in the development of reading skills. They also provide for many different reading abilities pupils need to acquire. A variety of materials are included. Among them are factual materials as well as fiction and poetry. In some cases, these are read for general impressions and in others they are for specific details or to get information for activities in other subject areas.

4. Do they provide for a worthwhile content? Most reading materials contain selections chosen for their value to children. The topics and ideas included are, insofar as possible, important for children to experience. There is frequently an attempt to relate these ideas with content presented in other subject areas.

Critical Questions:

Do the reading materials provide continuity of growth in reading skills, habits, and attitudes? How?

Do the reading materials provide for a wide variety of reading activities? In what way?

Is a complete organization of reading experiences provided?

Do the reading materials provide for a worthwhile content of ideas? How?

CONTROLS

Certain controls are used as guides in the construction and selection of reading materials. Research and experience provide a basis for using these controls. Not all materials available for the instructional reading program embody all controls, yet in extremely few cases are none of the controls utilized. The purpose of the controls is to provide materials of varying levels of difficulty. The controls supply a systematic basis for constructing and selecting appropriate materials for children with a wide range of reading skills and abilities.

Obviously, controls are devised to ensure that materials will contribute maximally to the reading program. These materials cover a wide range and many teachers do not use all of them. Some materials comprise the basic reading program (pre-primer, primer, and reader). Other materials are supplementary to the graded reading series (workbooks). A third type of material may be made a part of and contribute to the reading program (trade books, magazines, and newspapers).

Consensus is lacking on which of the controls are most important. Some analysts feel that one area of control is more important than any of the others, while other analysts choose a different control as most important. A few care very little for any of these controls.

There is disagreement as to the validity of these controls in measuring the difficulty of reading materials. Thus, each analyst must decide for himself which, if any, of the established measuring instruments he will use or if he will devise his own. For the most part, however, it is agreed that if and when controls are applied, they are most necessary in the early stages of the instructional program. As children become more competent in reading, it is believed that fewer controls are needed.

Not all of the controls outlined and briefly described in this section are compatible with each other. Each analyst must select the controls he believes are most important in materials used for instruction in reading and analyze the materials accordingly. It is obvious that difficulty will ensue if he selects controls diametrically opposed to each other. In such cases it will be necessary for him to re-evaluate the criteria he has been using to guide his work.

Six types of controls are presented in the remainder of this section:

1. *Vocabulary*. Vocabulary controls are used in materials for the reading program to make it possible for children to build a stock of sight words. Since a carefully controlled number of words is presented, repetition of these words is believed to help ensure their retention. Most basic reading materials have carefully controlled vocabularies. The following questions must be answered by each analyst for himself: are these basic words appropriate to the needs and interests of the children; is the number of basic words sufficient to provide enough story to retain the interest of children; is the amount of repetition likely to repel children; do words recur throughout the book or

series or do they tend to be presented intensively at one point and then not used again; are meaning and recognition of words developed together?

Supplementary materials frequently provide many activities designed to improve the reading vocabularies of children who use these materials. Among the activities included are: meaning and recognition drills; instruction in the use of the dictionary; teaching synonyms, antonyms, and homonyms; and learning uses of prefixes and suffixes. Vocabulary controls are probably most vigorously applied in materials prepared for beginners in the reading program.

2. *Phonics.* Phonics can be defined as the association of sounds with letters or combinations of letters. Much heat has been generated in discussions of the proper place of phonics in the reading program. This has been a major issue in the controversy concerning the most effective way of teaching reading.

Almost everyone believes that phonics is important in teaching children to read more effectively. The problem is to determine how much phonics, when it should be presented, which elements of phonics, to whom it should be presented, and in what ways it is most effectively provided.

Phonic controls are utilized in a somewhat different way from vocabulary controls. They are perhaps much more apparent and often tend to form a sub-program of reading instruction—a program within a program. In some relatively few cases, they are the program itself.

These questions need to be answered by the analyst: what portion of the materials is devoted to phonics; to what extent do phonics constitute a formal, systematic program of instruction; how is phonics integrated with other aspects of the reading program; and are the phonics principles clearly and accurately presented?

3. *Linguistic.* Some linguistic controls have long been employed in the preparation and selection of reading materials. However, until quite recently they have not been as prominent and have not been used as extensively or systematically as have other controls. The relatively late general recognition of the relationship between linguistic knowledge and reading has provided a new dimension to teaching reading. It has become the object of considerable interest and study as reading specialists have attempted to incorporate the most up-to-date linguistic knowledge in their reading programs and materials. The result has been a rapidly growing supply of materials with linguistic labels, plus a rather noticeable shift in emphasis in several established reading programs to meet the challenge of new programs with an openly declared linguistic orientation. Thus, the analyst must be prepared to scrutinize reading materials using linguistic controls. (For a more extended discussion of linguistic principles, see Chapter 6.)

Linguistic controls are concerned with regulating the structure of the language used in reading materials. This should not be confused with structural analysis, which is commonly used in teaching reading to mean the "unlocking" of unknown words by studying them for known root words and their inflectional endings and prefixes and suffixes. Linguistic controls as used in this discussion is a much broader, more inclusive term.

The analyst of reading materials may find the following questions useful in guiding his efforts: does the language structure in the reading materials move from simple to more complex, and is the level of complexity appropriate to the abilities of the children for whom the materials were prepared? Reading specialists have used these questions to assist them for many years. Children grow in their ability to understand and use language. They tend to experience difficulty and loss of interest if the language structure is too complex to be easily followed. This is especially true when they are attempting to master the basic skills of reading.

Are commonly used patterns of language employed in the materials? For most situations, real language is probably preferable to artificial, stilted language. Real language is that pattern of language commonly used in everyday life. Especially during the early stages of reading instruction, the language patterns in reading materials should, according to some experts, represent children's speech. Those are the patterns familiar and real to the children in the early grades.

4. *Concept.* The expansion of meaning is a primary responsibility of the school. This responsibility is met in many ways. Frequently it is done by deliberately providing children with reading materials that will develop and expand their concepts.

Concepts are abstractions. They exist only in the minds of people and thus go beyond what is immediately available to the senses. Words tend to become the labels for concepts. It should be noted, however, that concepts are intellectualizations of meanings of words, not the words themselves.

Concepts have their foundation in experience. They develop from experience and as more experience is gained and assimilated, concepts become broader and deeper. Concepts are complex, with many facets and dimensions. The meaning gained by an individual from his experience is a refinement and extension of his concepts.

In the reading program, the development of concepts is directly related to the meaning gained from the materials read. This is a much more complex process than it appears on the surface. Reading specialists have long been aware that concepts included in reading materials, both in number and level of complexity, are of tremendous importance in helping or hindering the reading development of children.

Analysts of reading materials will find that assessing reading materials on the basis of concept controls is a complex and difficult procedure. The questions and discussion provided in this section may make that task somewhat easier.

Is the concept load sufficiently restricted in materials prepared for use in the early stages of the instructional program so that children may concentrate on mastering basic reading skills? Reading specialists have long been concerned that the concept burden is too heavy for children learning to read. Concept burden is closely related to vocabulary. Unlike vocabulary controls discussed earlier, the emphasis here is on the meanings of words rather than the problems children have in recognizing and mastering new words (the printed symbols). If the reading materials contain a great many different words and/or many words that are not commonly used or heard by children in early grades, the chances are that the concept burden is heavy enough, at least, to distract children from the essential task of developing mastery of essential reading skills. The emphasis at this point is on reading as a skill, rather than on the use of reading to gain and expand meaning.

Are concepts smoothly and reasonably developed and extended in the reading materials? Children must possess a background of experience adequate for words contained in the reading material to accurately convey meaning. If children do not correctly connect words with experience, the result is misconception or verbalism. They can say a word, even use it correctly in speaking, and yet it might carry little or no meaning for them. Description may provide vicarious experience that extends meanings and helps define terms for the reader. Description is often provided by placing a term in context with other known and understood words. In other cases, longer descriptive passages or, indeed, a whole book may be used to give the necessary background of experience. It must be noted that one difficulty encountered by all children (and adults) is that many words have multiple meanings. When children learn more of the many meanings of words and fit these together in a coherent fashion, they are broadening and deepening their concepts. Many reading specialists believe that the analyst should study the materials for evidence that children are given reasonable help in learning new meanings of familiar words.

Is the concept level of the content appropriate to the children who are to use the reading materials? Concepts are not static; they may be broadened and deepened. Yet, logically, there is an optimum concept level for children at any stage in their development as readers. If the concept level goes beyond the ability of the children to handle it, there usually is a loss of interest, increased verbalism, or the development of misconceptions. If the concept level falls short of the degree of sophistication already attained by the children, the materials may be viewed as babyish, uninteresting, or trivial. One measure that the analyst may use in determining the appropriateness of concept level is the grade labels available for the reading materials. Another is a knowledge of the level of sophistication of the particular group of students the materials are being selected for. A third measure is the course of study used to guide teachers in school systems where the materials will be used. A fourth is knowledge, based on research, of reasonable expectations for children at different stages in their school careers.

5. *Interest.* Few classroom teachers or reading specialists

deny the significance of interest in promoting a desire to read—both more widely and more effectively. Much is known about the reading interests of elementary school children. Yet, there is not agreement on how to best use this knowledge.

Those who produce materials for reading programs almost always consider the interests of children as they prepare these materials. Some producers deliberately ignore what is known and choose to emphasize other controls in their materials. Most authorities agree that the analyst should be aware of available evidence of children's reading interests and the role these play in materials being considered for use in his situation.

There are two questions that will provide a focus for his scrutiny: do the materials parallel what is known about the reading interests of the children for whom they are designed? This can be a relatively simple process of matching materials with evidence already available. Are the materials designed to develop new interests in children? This is partly a matter of matching materials with what is known about children's interests. But the purpose of those who prepared the material is also important in the answer to this question. When the materials are *deliberately* designed to expand the reading interests of children, evidence is provided in two ways. The first is in a statement of purpose; the second is seen in the way the materials move from areas of known interest to new areas.

6. *Literary*. Literary controls are used to regulate the artistic features of the content presented in reading materials. (A more extensive discussion of literary principles is presented in Chapter 6.) This section presents three controls that may be useful to analysts of reading materials.

Is the content of high literary quality? For some reading specialists, this question may be answered in the affirmative if generous portions of the material consist of selections that have stood the test of time and are generally recognized to be of high literary quality. Other specialists take the position that materials are of high literary quality when the writer makes the experiences of which he writes come alive. He must be able to evoke feelings and emotions as well as excite the imagination. He makes it possible for the reader to live a richer, fuller life. In some cases, literary quality is believed to be of less consequence than other factors. The literary quality of the content of reading materials for beginning readers is not high. Vocabulary controls are believed to be more important in preparing these materials for children.

Is the content tastefully and artistically presented? This question is concerned with the appearance of the material. Esthetic qualities of illustrations, page arrangement, and other such matters are the focus of attention in applying this criterion. The intention is to draw children to the materials.

Do the materials contain a variety of selections so that children may become acquainted with many literary forms? Illustrations of the types of selections that might be included are factual and fictional materials and prose and poetry forms. The purpose of this criterion is to broaden the horizons of children by awakening them to the wide range of literary forms and how these may be used.

Critical Questions:

Do the reading materials embody vocabulary controls? If so, are the basic words appropriate to the needs and interests of children?

Is the number of basic words sufficient to provide enough story to retain the interest of children?

Is the amount of repetition sufficient to ensure retention? Is it likely to repel children?

Do words recur throughout the book or series or do they

tend to be presented intensively at one point and then not used again?

Are meaning and recognition of words developed together?

Do the materials contain phonic controls? If so, what portion of the material is devoted to phonics?

To what extent does phonics constitute a formal, systematic program of instruction?

How is phonics integrated with other aspects of the reading program?

Are the phonics principles clearly and accurately presented?

Do the reading materials include linguistic controls? If so, does the language structure in the reading materials move from simple to more complex?

Is the level of complexity appropriate to the abilities of the children the materials were prepared for?

Are commonly used patterns of language employed in the materials?

Do the reading materials employ concept controls? If so, is the concept load sufficiently restricted in materials prepared for use in the early stages of the instructional program, so that children may concentrate on mastering basic reading skills?

Are concepts smoothly and reasonably developed and extended in the reading materials?

Is the concept level of the content appropriate to the children who are to use the reading materials?

Do the reading materials embody interest controls? If so, do the materials parallel what is known about the reading interests of the children they are designed for?

Are the materials designed to develop new interests in children?

Do the reading materials include literary controls? If so, is the content of high literary quality?

Is the content tastefully and artistically presented?

Do the materials contain a variety of literary forms?

LEGIBILITY

Legibility, at first glance, seems to be a strange item in analyzing commercially prepared materials. However, legibility contributes markedly to the ease or efficiency with which a person reads. Both ease and efficiency are important in determining reading speed, and speed is one of the goals of the reading program after the basic skills are well developed.

Legibility in printed materials is determined by many of the same factors that are looked for in the legibility of handwritten materials. Among the more important of these Dechant includes the following:*

1. *Type size.* Type size is usually measured by the point, about a seventy-second of an inch. Appropriate size type for the developmental level of the pupil results in fewer fixations, fewer regressions, and a larger perception span. Speed is not an important factor in determining appropriate type size in the earlier grades. Emphasis at this stage is on comprehension—recognition and interpretation of what the student reads. Thus, speed is a relatively unimportant criterion in determining type size until about the fourth grade.

   Research indicates that type size should follow this pattern: grade one—between 14 and 18 points; grades two and three—between 12 and 14 points; upper grades—between 10 and 12 points.** Most adult readers prefer 9, 10, 11 or 12 point type.

---

* Emerald V. Dechant, *Improving the Teaching of Reading* (Englewood Cliffs, N.J.: Prentice-Hall, Inc., 1964), pp. 466–69.
** Miles A. Tinker, "Print for Children's Textbooks," *Education,* 80 (September 1959), 37–40; cited by Dechant, p. 466.

2. *Kinds of type.* "Studies generally have indicated that Roman print is more legible than italic type; lower case is more readable than typewriter type; and light face type is more legible than bold face."* This is a matter of preference of readers, rather than differences that enhance or hinder speed of reading.

3. *Distance between the lines of print.* In printing this is called the amount of leading. Optimum leading results in ease of reading and increases opportunities for greater reading speed. Usual leadings are: pre-primer—12 points; grade one—between 4 and 6 points; grade two—between 3 and 4 points; grades three and four—between 2 and 3 points; grades five and above—2 points.**

4. *Length of lines of print.* "When the lines are too short or too long, the reader tends to make more fixations and to read fewer words per fixation. Long lines make it more difficult to make the proper return sweep. Short lines lead to choppy reading because the eye does not use peripheral vision effectively."† The following line widths are recommended: grade one—$3\frac{1}{6}$ to $3\frac{1}{3}$ inches; grades two and three—$3\frac{1}{6}$ to $3\frac{2}{3}$ inches; grades four and above—$3\frac{1}{6}$ to 4 inches.‡ Adult readers prefer line lengths ranging from $2\frac{5}{6}$ to $4\frac{2}{3}$ inches.***

5. *Reflection of light by page.* Two elements are important for ease of seeing and, therefore, reading ease. Black print on light background is usually easier to read than other combinations. Generally, the surface of the paper should be rough enough to reduce glare to a minimum. The illumination provided will play

---

* Dechant, p. 466.
** *Ibid.,* pp. 466–67.
† *Ibid.,* pp. 467, 469.
‡ *Ibid.,* p. 468.
*** *Ibid.,* p. 467.

an important part in the matter of reflection. However, the materials themselves contribute greatly.

No one of these factors is by itself the most important consideration in determining legibility. Rather, all of them must be taken together.

Critical Questions:

Is the type size appropriate for the developmental stage of the children the materials are designed for?

Does the kind of type interfere with legibility?

Is the distance between lines of print within the range recommended for ease of reading?

Is the length of lines of print within the known range of preferences?

Is the reflection of light by the pages of the materials reduced to a minimum?

ASSOCIATED LEARNINGS

Reading is an integral part of the elementary school program. Learning and mastering reading skills are essential, but these skills are utilized in gaining information, other skills, habits, appreciations and attitudes in other parts of the school program. Reading is, in this sense, a skill subject. Its purpose is to enable children to learn effectively in all areas of study and to develop an interest in reading widely and deeply in many subjects.

In the process of learning to read, children are exposed to a great variety of ideas. It is impossible to learn to read without reading something. Constant awareness of this is imperative for teachers who would develop a sound reading program. Thus, it is generally agreed that a careful scrutiny of the content of reading materials is necessary. The following are principles for analyzing materials for associated learnings:

1. The informational content is relevant to the experiences of the pupils the materials are designed for. To

develop and sustain interest, the content must make sense to the pupils. It ought not be too far removed from what is familiar to them. The content should be related to what they know so as to be understood, believed, and used.

2. The information is adequate for use by these pupils. Adequacy is difficult to establish for children unless particular children are in mind. However, adequacy is measured in amount of content, usefulness to the children, and the appropriateness for the background of knowledge brought to it by the pupils.

3. The information is clearly and accurately presented. The method and style of presentation is important for clarity, as well as for acceptance by boys and girls. If it is condescending or pedantic or flowery, children tend to reject it. They generally prefer a straightforward and clear presentation. Accuracy is a prime consideration in analyzing nonfictional as well as fictional reading materials. Accuracy requires concentration on a true picture rather than overstressing the unique or sensational. Content should be abreast of the times, for this is also a matter of accuracy. Perhaps the answer to the following question will be of most help to the analyst: what do scholars in the field say about the accuracy and the up-to-dateness of the content?

4. The vocabulary and concepts are suitable to the age and interest level of the pupils and to the subject matter of the text. Provision for both of these at once is not always easy. It is frequently difficult for the analyst to see to it that materials selected are appropriate to the concept levels and interest levels of children while at the same time making sure that the subject matter is not distorted or attenuated to the extent that children are deprived of important and worthwhile information.

5. Explanations of technical terms or unfamiliar words necessary to the contents are provided as they are introduced. This is clearly related to other criteria just

mentioned. However, the point is that if understanding of content is important, there must be a real and successful effort to expand the vocabulary and concepts of children. Care must be taken to prevent technical terms, unfamiliar terms, from being presented without an effort to ensure understanding and, thus, learning.

Critical Questions:

Is the informational content relevant to the experiences of the pupils the materials are designed for?

Is the information contained in the materials adequate for these children?

Is the information clearly and accurately presented?

Are the vocabulary and concepts suitable to the age and interest level of the pupils and to the subject matter of the text?

Are explanations of technical terms or unfamiliar words necessary to the content provided as they are introduced?

SUITABILITY

Suitability is closely related to teachability. Both are of primary concern when analyzing materials for possible adoption in a *particular, known situation.* Suitability focuses on the relationship between the materials and the value orientation of the particular school, while teachability centers on the effectiveness of the materials in contributing to the reading program.

Decisions as to whether or not reading materials should be adopted in a particular school or system are based upon analyses of the materials in terms of certain principles:

1. Are the purposes, goals, or objectives of the materials compatible with the point of view of the adopting school? These goals are usually stated by the authors in the materials. The task of the analyst is to: deter-

mine the extent to which the authors reached these stated goals; find out if other unstated objectives are used in the materials; and compare these stated and unstated goals with the objectives of the teacher, school, or system he represents.

2. Are the materials in harmony with policies of the school? The content and style of the materials and suggestions for their use should probably be in agreement with plans and procedures of the teacher, school, or school system. When the discrepancy is too large, effective use of the materials is unlikely.

3. Are all facets of the reading program covered? Most reading authorities take the position that a variety of materials should be provided so that each child may be helped to grow in reading. All reading skills should be developed through the use of these materials.

4. Are the reading materials more economical than others that are available? In determining economy, many factors must be considered. Among them are the time expenditure required to do justice to these materials, their monetary cost, the effort and energy they require (from both teacher and pupil), and the general efficiency in assisting children to read more effectively.

5. Are the materials based upon the findings of sound research conducted in situations similar to that for which they are being considered for adoption? Put another way, it is the task of the analyst to determine that sufficient research evidence is presented to show that the materials have been used in classroom teaching situations and tested successfully. Since he is interested in selecting materials for a specific school or system, he will probably also want to check the conditions under which the research was conducted. It is particularly helpful to know that the materials have been tested in circumstances similar to those they are being considered for. When research data are limited,

of questionable validity, or non-existent, special care should be exercised in analyzing materials for suitability.

6. Are the reading materials correlated with the texts and materials in other areas of study? A degree of correlation is desirable for a number of reasons. The reading material may serve as a supplement to the learnings in other fields. Correlation can also lead to greater interest on the part of children. Correlation may provide a means for carryover of reading skills developed in the reading program.

Critical Questions:

Are the stated or implicit purposes, goals, or objectives of the materials compatible with the point of view of the adopting school?

Are the materials themselves in harmony with policies of the school?

Are all facets of the reading program covered?

Are the materials more economical than others that are available?

Are the materials based upon the findings of sound research conducted in situations similar to that for which they are being considered for adoption?

Are the reading materials correlated with the texts and materials in other areas of study?

TEACHABILITY

As indicated earlier, teachability has primarily to do with the effectiveness of the materials in contributing to the reading program. It might be phrased another way: Do the materials satisfy standards for effective instruction? The emphasis here is on the adequacy of these materials from the standpoint of instruction rather than of learning, internal consistency or other such factors.

To assess their teachability, the analysts must determine the extent to which the reading materials provide for:

1. Continuing the cultivation of readiness for new levels of skill development.

2. Building an ever larger reading vocabulary.

3. Developing greater skill in identifying unfamiliar words.

4. Giving impetus to wider reading beyond the basal materials.

5. Discovering and eliminating pupils' reading deficiencies.

6. Measuring pupil achievement.

7. Meeting individual differences in ability, skill, need and interest of children.

The analyst must also check the degree to which the materials supply a wide variety of selections and materials for pupils, and furnish adequate, clear instructional suggestions, as well as a coherent, valid pattern of suggested method that teachers might find helpful. Critical questions with regard to teachability may be drawn from the above statements.

SUMMARY

Educational principles have been developed through research, experience, and logic. Those responsible for selecting reading materials must make their choices from among many possibilities. Knowledge of educational principles will enable these educators to systematically analyze the materials to determine which are most appropriate for their school programs. These educational principles are grouped under the following headings: sequence, scope, and integration; controls; legibility; associated learnings; suitability; and teachability.

Principles of sequence, scope, and integration are concerned with the provisions for continuity of growth in reading, wide variety of reading activities, complete organization of reading experiences, and worthwhile content of ideas. Controls provide a basis for systematically constructing and selecting materials appropriate for children of greatly varying reading skills and abilities. Six types of control were discussed: vocabulary, phonics, linguistic, concept, interest, and literary. The ease and efficiency of reading are influenced by the legibility of the reading materials. Type size, kind of type, distance between lines, width of lines of print, and reflection of light from the page contribute markedly to the legibility of the materials.

Associated learnings are those derived from the content of reading materials. The content should be examined to determine its relevance to the experiences of children, adequacy of information for children's use, clarity and accuracy of presentation, suitability of vocabulary and concepts to the age and interests of children, as well as to the subject matter, clarity, completeness, and timeliness of explanations of technical vocabulary and unfamiliar words. Suitability focuses on the relationship between the materials and the value orientation of a particular school. The analyst may use the following points to guide him in evaluating the suitability of reading materials: compatibility of stated and unstated objectives of the materials with those of the teacher, school or system; harmony of the materials with school policies; completeness of the reading program provided by the materials; economy of the materials; sufficiency of research evidence supporting the use of the materials; and adequacy of correlation with materials and texts in other subject areas. Teachability is concerned with the effectiveness of the materials in advancing the instructional program in reading. Among the factors contributing to the teachability of materials are the variety of selections and materials included, the program provided to develop reading skills, and the instructional suggestions and pattern of suggested method furnished for teachers.

Chapter 5

Linguistic
Principles

Reading is one of four phases of communication. Communication always has a sending phase and a receiving phase; there are at least two persons engaged in complementary occupations during communication. In oral communication the speaker attempts to convey a message to the listener who actively seeks to understand. In written language, the writer seeks to convey a message to the reader who actively seeks to understand.

The symbols in the one case are sounds, in the other they are letters or other graphic forms. The sensory input is different, but the process by which the listener or reader understands is much the same.

In recent years the scientific understanding of language, its units, and the systems which fit the units together to communicate meaning have increased dramatically. More recently, linguists, educationists, and others have sought to apply this knowledge of language to the teaching of reading. They have sought to develop linguistically valid methods and materials.

To be considered linguistically valid, reading materials must be consistent with accurate knowledge of language and how it functions in communication.

WHAT IS LINGUISTICS?

Linguistics is the scientific study of language. Linguists have staked out a domain in the pursuit of knowledge and have developed terminology, methodology and, most important, an expanding body of scientific findings.

In general, the linguist, as a scientist, attempts to operate free from prejudgments. He takes language as he finds it, seeking to describe how it works and not force preconceived patterns upon it. The linguist accepts oral language as primary; *the* language is what its users speak.

Descriptive linguistics is a term often used to differentiate the linguist's approach from the prescriptive approach of traditional grammarians. The latter consider a body of grammatical rules to exist quite independently of the way language is spoken at any time or place: "It's me" is wrong even if every cultured user were to say it.

Several fields are closely allied to linguistics in the pursuit of knowledge about language. Communications theory is concerned with the whole communication process. Language is viewed by communication theorists as a complex code composed of symbols with no meaning of their own. An encoder uses the code to transmit a message to a decoder. Communications theory is concerned with the means and efficiency of the code in transmitting information.

Psycho-linguistics is concerned with the complex inter-relationships between language and thought processes. Basically, the process of reading is a psycho-linguistic one since it involves comprehension.

Linguistic terminology. Every field of inquiry sharpens its concepts and uses terms to express its concepts in precise ways. Sometimes these terms are familiar ones given more precise definition. Sometimes new terms are created to express new relationships as the field creates knowledge.

Linguistics as a rapidly growing field has been developing such a set of terms. Educators should be careful to note the special precise meaning to the linguist of terms more loosely used by the general public. They should be cautious about equating new terms with old ones. In most cases, new terms express new concepts which differ in important ways from older concepts.

Some important terms needed to discuss linguistic criteria for reading materials follow:

Phonemes: Phonemes are bundles of sounds closely related in important ways and differing in ways not significant for the language. Sounds can be produced by humans in almost infinite variety. But only a limited number of phonemes or bundles of sounds are used in the language. In the same way that a bundle of colors in the spectrum may be all considered red, a bundle of sounds may be all considered /b/. The units of any language are not sounds but phonemes, since users will accept any sound which falls within certain limits of variation as /b/. A native speaker will tend, in fact, not to notice differences between sounds within a phoneme but hear them as identical. "Spin" and "pin" seem to contain a common sound /p/. Actually, the /p/ in "pin" is accompanied by an explosion of air and /p/ in "spin" is not. In English this is not a significant difference. But the initial sounds in "pin" and "bin" are different in a significant way which is readily noticeable. Phonemes have no meaning of their own. Only when they are strung together in a sequence can they begin to represent meaning.

Morphemes: A morpheme is a molecule of language, the smallest unit which has characteristics of the language itself. It can carry meaning. Two forms of morpheme are (1) free forms which can occur alone, and (2) bound forms which must be attached to free morphemes. "Talk" is a free morpheme, while "ing," "s," "ed" are bound forms.

The linguist usually prefers to talk about *morphemes*

rather than *words*. The *word* concept is not easy to define in a consistent way.

Morphemes may carry lexical, or dictionary, meanings, but only in the flow of language do they have their full meaning because the context always contributes to meaning.

Inflection: Changes which take place in words, or by adding bound morphemes that produce changes in meaning or range of use, are inflectional changes. Inflection is less important in English than it once was or than it is in other languages. We inflect nouns to some extent (as "tent," "tents"; verbs to a greater degree ("look," "looks," "looked," "looking"); adjectives and adverbs hardly at all "big," "bigger," "biggest"). The way we show past tense is by an inflectional change as when "I walk home" becomes "I walked home." We say "he walks home" but "they walk home."

Syntax: Syntax is the system by which morphemes are combined to produce patterns of language fully capable of transmitting meaning. In English, pattern is very important in establishing meaning. Every language utilizes a limited number of morphemic patterns of arrangement of the morphemes. "John hit Jim" is a very common pattern. The position of "John" and "Jim" convey to the reader who was the aggressor and who received the blow. Only on the syntactic level does language really become a means of communication, because the *lexical meaning* of the morphemes must be supplemented by *contextual meanings* for a whole sentence to be meaningful. The basic syntactical patterns are used consistently by all children by the time they begin school.

Function or structure words. There are a small number of words in the English language (about 200) that should more properly be called signals than words. They have little or no lexical meaning but they play important roles in making language communicate meaning. In this question, "did John hit Jim," one would have a hard time assigning any meaning to "did," but the whole phrase is changed from the positive statement used earlier to a question. "Did" is functioning here as a *question marker*. Words such as "the," "a," "an," "this," "one," and "five" function as *noun markers*. "In," "on," "to," "for," "of" exercise the function of *phrase markers*. "Not" signals negation of a positive statement.

Two things about function words are important in reading: 1. They occur with great frequency in the language. About one-third of the flow of language is composed of function words. It is, therefore, virtually impossible to avoid their use in even the earliest reading materials. 2. The spelling of many function words does not follow regular patterns. Examples are: "is," "was," "were," "a," "the," "what," "who," "do," "to," "from," "of," "above," "can," "done."

Intonation. In oral language, stress, pitch, and pause (or juncture) play vital roles in the meaning of sentences and phrases. These are aspects of the intonation of language. Most people are aware of special intonation which can give special emotional loadings to common statements. "I like you" can take on a variety of special meanings when different intonations are applied. But there are important intonation aspects of language that are necessary regardless of any special emotional loading. The end of every statement is signalled by an intonational package called a phrase terminal intonation. A rise or fall in pitch, a succession of stresses of variable intensity, and pauses of differing duration and finality tell us whether we are to keep listening, respond to a question, or do something in response to a request.

The relationship between the words of a sentence are vitally influenced by intonation. "That man is a criminal lawyer." Is he a lawyer who deals with the laws of crime or is he a criminal himself? The relative stresses of "criminal" and "lawyer" make this clear in the spoken language.

Written language can only partially express intonation with white space and a few punctuation marks.

Graphemes. Linguists, in speaking of written language, have coined the word "grapheme," which they prefer to use rather than "letter." A grapheme is more of a perceptual category than a real thing. The grapheme <A> can be written in a number of very different ways: the common printed capital, small printed forms which exist in several variations, the circle and line manuscript small letter, and a variety of cursive capitals and small letters which differ stylistically and differ also depending on other letters they are joined to.

The child must know that <A> in "All" is equal to <a> in "all' and <ɑ> in "ɑll." Later he must learn that <A> in "All" and <a> in "all" are also forms of the same grapheme. "All," "all," "all," "All," "all" must be read as being the same; the differences must be ignored. The grapheme is composed of a variety of forms which must be perceived by the reader as equivalent, just as a phoneme is composed of a variety of sounds which must be perceived by the listener as equivalent.

Grapheme-phoneme correspondence. The alphabetic system of writing is based on representing sounds by letters. If English orthography followed this principle consistently there would be complete grapheme-phoneme correspondence. Each grapheme would consistently represent a single phoneme and only that phoneme. This correspondence is of course far from perfect.

Several graphemes or combinations of graphemes may represent one phoneme as: "too," "do," "you," "flue," "chew." Similarly, one grapheme may represent several different phonemes as does "s" in "sure," "since," "saves." In island, "s" represents no phoneme.

Every science is characterized by areas of broad agreement among authorities and frontier areas in which conflicting theories and positions exist side by side. Linguistics is not an exception. The branch of linguistics known as phonemics, the study of the phonemes of language, has achieved the greatest agreement (though this is not yet complete). At the other extreme, syntax is an area of great disagreement. Linguists have not yet completely agreed on a common terminology. Some might say that application of linguistics could wait for greater agreement. This would, however, be analogous to suggesting that Columbus ought to have waited until geographers had resolved whether the earth was round or flat before setting out on his voyage.

ACCURACY OF LANGUAGE INFORMATION

Linguists, and others conversant with linguistics, are raising two related questions about materials for teaching reading. The first question, are the reading materials built on valid linguistic principles? is the general one to which this chapter is addressed. It will be considered through a series of sub-questions later. But a more specific question may be asked: is the language information contained in the reading material consistent with scientific knowledge? This language information as *content,* that is, as the subject of instruction, is presented in three ways: as information for the teacher (presented in a teacher's manual or special teacher's edition of the material); as information for direct instruction of pupils (presented either in sections following story material, special materials or a variety of other ways);

and in the form of exercises. These exercises are either designed to demonstrate language information already presented or they are designed to lead the child to discover language information.

While no one would argue with the desirability of having accurate information about language in reading material as compared with inaccurate information, there are some related issues on which there is no such agreement.

Linguists criticize most language information contained in current reading materials on phonics as based on inaccurate, unscientific descriptions of the sounds of the language. They also lament artificial language and unusual language patterns in reading materials. How one reacts to these criticisms depends on whether one accepts certain basic assumptions of linguistics. Is the oral language *the* language (as compared to the literary form found only in formal written English)? Is the source of language knowledge a scientific description of the oral language of contemporary users (or is it prescriptive writings by language authorities)? Is there one correct English which must be presented and used at all times in reading materials? Are there correct ways to say words? Is there a correct vowel sound in "frog," correct no matter where the speaker lives, or is one sound correct in Chicago and another in New York?

Another question some would raise is, why is language information presented at all? A large body of research can be cited which shows that there is no significant relationship between language information and reading ability. Those who raise this question might agree that the teacher needs to know about language, but they would argue that teaching children about language as a means of improving their reading is a waste of time, which could be better spent in more reading.

Critical Questions:

What language information is provided for the teacher?

Is language information provided for direct instruction to the pupil?

Are exercises provided which confirm or present language information?

What is the source of language information?

Is the language information presented consistent within itself?

Is the language information presented consistent with scientific knowledge of language?

PHONEMIC CONSIDERATIONS

Leonard Bloomfield, an early giant among linguists, first explored the possibility of constructing reading materials which were controlled in such a way that only words with regular grapheme-phoneme (g-p) correspondence were used. In all words introduced, each grapheme always represented one phoneme and that one only. No words were introduced which had a grapheme that represented a phoneme it did not usually represent. Through this control the one-symbol-for-one-phoneme goal could be achieved artificially by postponing until later introduction of words with irregular correspondence. Some have suggested that nonsense syllables could be used in reading material in preference to real words since the child could focus on learning the g-p correspondence and not be distracted by meaning.

Phonics programs are also based on attempts at teaching generalizations about relationships between letters and sounds in words. The goal of these programs is to enable children to sound out new words. Phonics programs are not usually based on linguistics. Children are often taught in phonics programs that letters have sounds. Linguists prefer to say letters *represent* sounds.

Another approach to achieving high correspondence between sound and symbol is the Initial Teaching Alphabet (ITA). This alphabet is designed to represent each phoneme in English with a distinctive grapheme (which in this case would have only one variant since there are no capitals). ITA is to be used in reading materials and writing activities until a point, perhaps in the third grade for most children, when a transition is made to traditional orthography. The ITA symbols, by intent, look very similar to the letters they generally replace.

Charles Fries, the well-known American linguist, has suggested another approach to constructing reading materials, based on the relationship between minimal contrasts in groups of words and minimal contrasts in the spelling patterns in the written representation of these words. For example, the group of words: "rat," "hat," "fat," "mat," "slat," would be contrasted with "rate," "hate," "fate," "mate," "slate." The intent is not to teach direct g-p correspondence but to teach the relationship between patterns of graphemes and patterns of phonemes. The emphasis is on learning to discriminate minimal contrasts.

There are, of course, negative views on all of these approaches. Some would, in fact, say that the child's primary focus when learning to read should be on whole words or syntactical units. They might argue that reading materials designed to teach children g-p correspondence which they will then apply in reading are based on the assumption that transfer of training will take place. This assumption some would question, since similar transfer of training generally has not been found in research studies.

An argument of central importance in the value of teaching generalizations about sound and symbol relationship is the great irregularity in English spelling. Some say that this irregularity is so great that no generalizations are reliable enough to be worth teaching. Others minimize the significance of the irregularity, pointing instead to the large percentage of English words which are spelled regularly.

Critical Questions:

What provision is made for controlling grapheme-phoneme correspondence?

Is this provision consistent throughout the materials?

Is irregularity introduced in a planned and systematic way?

Are spelling patterns used in building the materials?

Are spelling patterns used consistently?

Are phonics (sound-symbol) generalizations taught as such in the materials?

MORPHEMIC CONSIDERATIONS

Linguists talk about words but they prefer to deal with morphemes because they find the word concept an elusive one. Adults are used to thinking about words as self-evident, and indeed in graphic form they are since they are neatly marked off by white space. In speech we also mark off many words with pauses, but these pauses do not neatly coincide with the graphic white spaces. How is the child to know that "away" is one word but "have to" is two words? On close examination words are not the obvious entities we normally consider them. Yet words are the central focus of many early reading programs.

Words are frequently handled outside of language context through word lists, flash cards, word charts, and other devices. When words are read in lists they all have the same intonation, one that seldom occurs on single words in the flow of language. The pronunciation of words in isolation may also be unreal. For instance "the," "a," "have" will tend to be pronounced on lists in ways which are not the most common ones in language. In "the man" or "a man" or in "have to," we have common pronunciations which differ markedly from the list forms.

Another concept from linguistics that must be considered is that of allologues (alternate forms of words). Cultured users of English frequently prefer to use contractions to full forms. Thus they say "I'm coming" rather than "I am coming" in many situations and "I don't think so" instead of "I do not think so." Reading materials based on controlled vocabulary may inadvertently produce stilted language if contractions are avoided.

Recent psycho-linguistic research indicates that children acquire inflectional suffixes at an early age, well before they begin learning to read in school. Children are not likely to read "sees" incorrectly if it occurs with a noun that takes the "s" form, as in "he sees me." Furthermore, children will have also learned what sound the plural morpheme takes when combined with words ending in various sounds. They will say "dogs," "watches," "cats," and "classes." This suggests that the common avoidance of "s" forms in early reading material is not necessary.

Derivational suffixes appear, however, to be learned much later. Many school-age children will say "the hunting man," or "the man who was hunting," rather than "the hunter." Derivational suffixes are not very common or important in English, which may explain why this acquisition is delayed in children. Special attention in reading materials may be necessary when derivational suffixes are introduced.

Critical Questions:

What focus is there in the reading material on words as such?

Is any assistance offered to the pupil in delineating words

and developing a concept of what words are? Are words presented and taught in isolation? If so, how are the problems of intonation and pronunciation handled?

What attention is given to compound words?

How are inflectional and derivational suffixes handled in the material?

Are contractions used in places where adults would normally use them, or are contractions avoided?

SYNTACTIC CONSIDERATIONS

As indicated, words have meaning only in the context of language. Larger language units, sentences and groups of sentences include all of the elements needed to convey meaning. These are pattern, function words, inflectional endings and agreement between the inflectional endings of words in the sentence, and intonation.

The studies of Strickland and Loban have indicated that all syntactic patterns of English are present in the speech of kindergarten and first-grade children. The children have learned to use the cue systems present in sentence structures to get meaning from oral language. It would follow that if the same structures are present in their reading materials, they will be able to use the same system of cues. One study has shown, in fact, that even first-graders find it easier to read words in stories than from lists where syntactical cues are lacking.

A key question then is whether reading materials contain the common syntactical structures of oral language; a related question is whether the patterns in reading materials occur in roughly the same frequency as they do in oral language. Strickland found that the most common pattern in basal readers she examined did not occur at all in the speech of children in her study (this pattern is the "look, said mother," or object-verb-subject type).

One way to guarantee close correspondence between the

syntax of the reading material and the syntax of the oral language as the child knows it, is to use the language of children, written down, as reading material. This, of course, is just what happens in experience stories, if they are accurately transcribed. Another procedure those constructing reading material may use is to consciously and continuously attempt to use "real language."

Another possibility in constructing reading materials is to move from simple common patterns to complex uncommon ones. "I see you" is a very simple example of the most common English pattern, subject-verb-object. "The boy who lives down the block and sells newspapers after school was secretly observing the pretty little girl who sits next to him in class," is an example of a complex use of the same common pattern. "The boy who lives down the block and sells newspapers after school" fills the same position (or slot) as "I" in "I see you." "Was secretly observing" fills the verb slot. "The pretty little girl who sits next to him in class" is the filler of the subject slot in this subject-verb-object pattern. On the other hand, "see Pepper run" is a very unusual pattern used in a way that is much more complex than its brevity would indicate. "Run" rather than "runs" following a third person singular verb is correct but rare. The pattern itself is unusual. Loban found in his study that children at different ages used the same patterns but varied considerably in the fillers of the slots in those patterns. More skilled users of language used more dependent clauses and more conditionality. It follows that the more complex the fillers of basic patterns become, the more difficult the reading material will become.

Attention can be given in reading materials to the contextual settings of commonly confused words. "Was" and "saw" are commonly interchanged by children learning to read, for example. This confusion will not take place in language structure where only one and not the other could be compatible with the other cues in the structure. Either could fit the slot in this pattern: "the man——John." But in this pattern only "saw" makes sense: "the man ——the woman." And in this sentence only "was" fits: "I——going to the store."

The handling of function words is another basis for analyzing reading materials. These words are very important to the meaning of sentences but have little meaning of their own. It has long been known that these words are the hardest for children to learn as isolated words. Children continually confuse "the," "this," "that" but easily learn "something," "surprise," and other less common words. One solution would be always to present these words in stories or at least in phrases accompanying the types of words they are most commonly associated with. Thus, instead of labeling a picture "house," it could be labeled "a house" or "the house." The dilemma, of course, is that these words are needed early in learning to read, but they are hard to learn. Another solution is to intensify drill on these words with flash cards, word games, and exercises. This latter approach treats function words as hard to learn words rather than as special category words almost void of referential meaning.

Critical Questions:

Is the language of the reading material real language, similar to the oral language as the learner knows it?

Do reading materials contain the common language structures of oral language?

Do these structures occur in the same frequency as in oral language?

Is any attempt made to proceed from common to uncommon language structures?

Is any attempt made to proceed from simple to complex fillers of the slots in language structures?

Is structural and contextual ambiguity avoided?

How are function words handled in reading materials?

Are there any special efforts in the reading material to present syntactic cues in reading?

Is any special effort made in teacher materials to assist him in helping children to use syntactic cues?

INTONATION CONSIDERATIONS

Intonation is represented only incompletely in written language through punctuation. The reader himself must supply the intonational cues which are missing. Reading materials can be constructed to help the reader infer intonation from punctuation and to supplement this with the full intonational melody which would be present in oral language.

Traditionally, the teaching of punctuation has been part of the writing program. Children were taught to end a sentence with a period. To do this, however, the child needs to know what a sentence is. To tell him that a sentence is a complete thought is to supply him with an abstraction which he may not be ready for. He has, however, as an infant learned to recognize a pattern of phrase terminal intonations which signals the end of a statement. One approach to teaching him to use punctuation is to associate the graphic punctuation mark, in this case the period, with the intonational signal he already uses.

Many teachers have intuitively been encouraging children to supply their own intonational cues by urging them to read "with expression" or to "read it the way you would say it to a friend on the playground." In doing this teachers have at least recognized the emotive function of special intonations. Reading materials can make them aware of the more general relationship of intonational signals to meaning.

Critical Questions:

Do the reading materials relate punctuation to intonation?

Are children encouraged to supply the natural intonations in reading?

Does the material assist the teacher in understanding how intonation functions in communication?

Does the material assist the teacher in helping children achieve natural intonations?

DIALECT CONSIDERATIONS

In Chapter 3, aspects of dialect were considered as they related to the experience, values, and cultural background of the learner. In this chapter we are more concerned with the language aspects.

Every dialect of a language has its own phonemic structure, morphemic stock, and syntactical system. These have been deeply internalized by the child when he comes to school. From the linguist's point of view, it is a serious mistake to regard one dialect as a low or ungrammatical form of another. Dialects of English have many similarities but they also have many differences. These differences tend to be systematic. The speaker of a certain dialect does not add "r" to certain words. He pronounces the word differently from the speaker of another dialect because he has a different set of phonemes.

Similarly, a "frying pan" to one may be a "skillet" to another and a "spider" to a third. One name is not more correct than the other except within a particular dialect.

But there is only one accepted system of spelling in American English (which differs in some minor ways from the English spellings). Regardless of how we pronounce "frog," we all spell it the same. There is no southern spelling different from midwestern or New England spelling. The point is that if each child learns to read his own language, the relationship between graphic symbols and oral language varies from dialect to dialect. If, on the other hand, only one relationship between oral and written language is considered "correct," then the child who does not speak the correct dialect is penalized and may be quite confused. If a child sees "four" and can only satisfy his teacher and the author of his reading material by a midwestern response, though he has long since come to associate a quantitative concept with the language label "fo'," it is possible he may recognize neither word nor concept. Even if he does make the connection he is given the double task of learning a new dialect and learning to read at the same time.

In this discussion we have pointed up two very different approaches to the problem of dialect in learning to read. One approach is that there is a correct English and that all language instruction, including reading, must utilize and insist on correct English. The other is that learning to read and learning a preferred dialect are entirely separate tasks.

Within the first approach several choices are possible. Reading materials can: 1. Provide the teacher with background to understand digerences between the dialects of the learners and the "correct" dialect. 2. Include in the reading readiness phase a program of teaching the "correct" dialect to the learners. They would learn to speak the new dialect first and then learn to read. 3. Ignore the problem entirely on the assumption that dialect differences are not an important deterrent to reading learning.

Within the second approach several choices are possible. ground to understand differences between the dialects of the learner. Words would be spelled conventionally, but vocabulary and syntax would be based in the readers' dialect. 2. Provide the teacher with the background necessary to understand what language behavior of children is dialect based and not immature language. The teacher would then be encouraged to let children read the way adult speakers in their language communities might speak. 3. Provide opportunities for learners to widen the range of language which they understand. This would involve a planned expansion outward from the child's own language to the comprehension of the dialects of others. Eventually it could lead to a shift in personal language toward a dialect which the child would come to recognize as preferred.

Critical Questions:

Do the reading materials assume a single "correct" English?

Do the materials for the teacher and the child separate learning to read from learning a preferred dialect?

Are dialect differences recognized? How?

Is there provision for dialect differences in the materials? How?

Is any attempt made to change oral language: prior to reading instruction; concurrently with reading instruction?

Is there any attempt to widen the range of language comprehension and use?

What assistance, if any, is given the teacher in understanding dialect problems in reading?

GENERAL LINGUISTIC CONSIDERATIONS

In addition to the specific areas of linguistic analysis we have cited there are some general linguistic principles which can be applied to reading materials.

Relationship of material to child language. A growing body of research is emerging on child language. The term "child language" is preferred to "children's language" because researchers have come to view the language of the child as something unique, not the child's version of the adult language but a distinct language having characteristics of its own.

Strong positions have not yet emerged on what the relationship should be between child language and materials for helping children become literate. One factor which those constructing reading materials need to consider is the developmental nature of all language learning. There is apparent in studies of child language development a movement through stages to language which fits within adult norms. Closer and closer approximation to adult norms characterizes this developmental process. But perfection by adult standards is not achieved at once. One approach which reading materials can incorporate is to continuously present language models consistent with adult norms and always judge children's performance on a scale of adult perfection.

An alternate approach is to bring reading materials more into accord with child language and accept imperfection, error, and language experimentation as part of the process of increasing approximation of adult norms.

Still other views are possible, but in any case the developmental nature of child language and the common characteristics of the language of children will require some response in building reading materials.

Child's language knowledge. The child learning to read his native language is learning to read a language he already speaks quite fluently. To some this means that the reading program and reading materials must put the pre-existing language knowledge of the child to work in making him literate. They argue that reading material must contain language as the child knows it. The authors of reading material must be aware of the devices in language which the child has learned to respond to. The child is already responding on a highly internalized level to the patterns, inflections, function words, sounds, and intonational melodies of the oral language. To what extent does a given set of reading materials tap this knowledge and draw on it?

Meaning in reading materials. How meaning is handled in reading materials comes close to initial assumptions that every writer of reading materials is forced to make when he defines reading. Already mentioned is a view of reading which focuses on breaking the grapheme-phoneme code. Reading for this group is learning to associate sounds with letters. Written language is a kind of continuous rapid cryptogram. The reader exchanges sounds for letters, then reconstructs oral language, and only then proceeds to the message. In this view meaning can be totally ignored in early reading materials since it is the decoding skill that is being taught.

At the opposite end of the continuum is the definition of reading as deriving meaning from the printed page. Comprehension of a message is an integral part of reading by this definition and, in fact, there can be no reading without meaning, even in the earliest material. Everything presented to a child to read, according to this view, must have something to say within the scope of the child's experience and conceptual ability. Only whole language units and groups of sentences can convey meaning. Learning grapheme-phoneme correspondences and learning the names of words (word-calling) are subsidiary skills, but they are not reading unless the child understands at some level.

Most popular basal readers which are built on the basis of controlled vocabulary begin with a vocabulary too small to adequately present full and varied meanings. They use pictures, therefore, to add precise definition to words where syntax and context are too sparse to accomplish this. The pictures also serve as the situational context of the words themselves, so that the child uses a combination of picture and language cues to get meaning.

More advanced reading materials will differ less than beginning materials since all approaches recognize that the ultimate goal of reading instruction is to produce readers who can read a wide variety of written and printed materials with understanding. But these advanced materials will still reflect pronounced differences over whether skills are treated as ends or means.

Redundancy. From communications theory comes a new view of a phenomenon which has been noted by others, but which acquires new importance because of this new view. There are forty-four phonemes in English. Limited as this number is, the possible sequences in which they could theoretically be combined becomes very large. But of these possible sequences, many do not occur at all in the language. Any native speaker of the language can tell that a combination of phonemes does not sound like English. The sequence is not permissible by rules we all accept. Some sequences occur only at initial, medial, or final positions in words. On the other hand, a few sequences occur with very great frequency in all positions. There is similar constraint on sequences of graphemes, morphemes, words and patterns, inflectional endings and syntactic ones. This constraint is a characteristic of all known languages. Communications theorists point out that this constraint on possible sequences cuts down the amount of information which each unit of language can communicate. They use the term redundancy to describe the inefficiency of language.

But from the view of listener or reader, redundancy is a boon. He can predict from his language experience what is likely to follow what in language. He is thus propelled onward. He already has some notion of what comes next before he hears or sees it. A missed cue is not so vital because other redundant cues are available. In "the boys eat their lunches at noon," only certain letters can follow "t" or precede "he." After an initial "t," letters such as "n," "m," "p," "q" cannot occur. Only certain words can precede "boys" or follow "the." If "boys" has the "s" inflection then "eat" must not have it, and the possessive pronoun must be "their" and not "his." (All these cues convey only a single bit of information; the plural nature of the subject.)

Some attempts have been made to measure redundancy in reading materials and compare this to the redundancy in child and adult language, but the use of redundancy as a factor in insuring readability in reading materials has not been explored much as yet.

Experience stories, faithful to the language of children, would be likely to contain the same redundancy as the language they are based on.

Critical Questions:

Is the reading material based on child language?

Does the reading material reflect the view that language learning is developmental?

Is the teacher provided with help in understanding child language and child language development?

Does the material draw on the prior language knowledge of the learners?

Does the material help the teacher draw on the prior language knowledge of the learner?

What definition of reading is stated or implicit in the reading materials?

Are early reading materials meaningful?

If so, is the meaning within the range of experience and conceptual development of the learners?

Are pictures used to cue meaning?

Are skills implicitly or explicitly regarded as ends or means in the materials?

Is redundancy considered in constructing the material?

Do the reading materials correspond in redundancy to the oral language of children?

SUMMARY

New materials for teaching reading are beginning to appear which claim to be linguistic, or to utilize "the linguistic method." In this chapter we have presented some linguistic terminology and concepts and discussed their application to reading.

The accuracy of language information presented or implicit in reading materials can be judged linguistically.

Phonemic, morphemic, syntactic, and intonational aspects may be some basis for reading materials. The varied dialects of readers may or may not be provided for in reading materials.

Some general linguistic considerations in reading materials are: the relationship of reading material to child language, how the child's language knowledge is tapped, how meaning is handled, and how language redundancy is used.

Linguistic considerations take on perspective when it is remembered that readers read language. Linguistics is the science of language.

Chapter 6

Literary

Principles

WHAT IS LITERATURE?

Whether literature is defined broadly or narrowly, most of what is found in nearly all materials designed for teaching reading is literature. Viewed another way, the basic *content* of *most* reading materials for children is literature.

Broadly defined, almost anything expressed in written language could be included as literature. A more narrow definition requires aesthetic value in written language and artistic use of language before it is considered literature. In this chapter, the more limited definition of literature will be employed. Even so, literature includes fiction and nonfiction, material read for information and material read for pleasure, prose and poetry, folklore, fantasy, and true-to-life stories; it has many forms and types.

READING MATERIALS NOT LITERATURE

In two very opposite views, materials for teaching reading are not considered as literature. In the first view, teaching reading is considered as the teaching of a series of skills which must be learned *before* the child can attempt to read literature. The reading materials involve exercises designed to teach some of the following: the alphabet, phonics, phoneme-grapheme correspondences, spelling pattern contrasts, sight vocabulary, and word-attack skills. Which of these are taught will depend on which skills are considered prerequisite in the reading program. In an extreme application, all skills would be taught in isolation and never in relationship to anything resembling literature. Such extreme programs are rare. More common is a plan of moving into literature usually near the end of the first year's work in reading.

The second view is that literature does not exist for the purpose of teaching reading. In this view, by definition, any material which is specially prepared, adapted, or controlled for the purpose of reading instruction is not literature; literature is somehow corrupted if it is used to teach reading.

Some authorities believe an appreciation of literature is not likely to be encouraged by the kinds of laborious analysis and practice which often accompany the use of reading materials. Literature, it is pointed out, should be read for pleasure, without the distractions and interruptions which are unavoidable in the acquisition of reading skills and abilities.

Though these two views are poles apart, the end result is the same. Literary principles are considered irrelevant to the materials used in teaching reading.

One critical question must precede all others that relate to literary principles: is the reading material based on a view of reading instruction in which literary principles are relevant?

INSTRUCTIONAL MATERIALS AS A SPECIAL FORM OF LITERATURE

Another view is that reading materials constitute a special form of literature, a modified form in which literary principles are relevant but less significant than other considerations. If the content can be simplified and controlled according to key criteria and still be good literature, so much the better. But the literary quality takes a back seat.

Literary characteristics of the content are viewed not as

values in themselves but as a kind of sugar-coating to make the learning of reading a more attractive and interesting task. Particularly in the first years of reading instruction, such goals as gaining appreciation for literature and developing taste in literature are far down the list of objectives or not on it at all.

If literary quality is a secondary consideration, then inclusion of characters children can identify with, concern for children's interests, provision for variety in form and type are basically devices to promote reading learning, not literary principles applied for their own sake.

To some extent also, publishers of instructional reading material may be concerned with creating a product which appeals to school personnel, particularly teachers. Literary devices and attention to literary principles may not be directly involved in the reading program but may be part of the publisher's attempt to market an attractive product.

In some programs for teaching reading and in upper grade materials of most programs, literature takes on an importance of its own. If the basic goal of the instructional program is not just to teach children basic reading skills but to teach them to read language for meaning, then the materials used in the program must be viewed as literature and held up to examination according to literary principles.

Critical Questions:

Are instructional reading materials viewed as a special form of literature?

Are literary qualities of the content ends in themselves or means to facilitate learning of skills?

CONTENT

It must be remembered, as one examines the content of reading materials, that the "stories" may or may not embody characteristics commonly associated with literature.

Some materials, written for the purpose of simplifying the task of learning to read, are viewed by their authors as tools for learning. No attempt has been made to vary the content presented or to insure that it is of high literary quality.

Other authorities point out that what children read, whether designed as material for practice or not, becomes part of the curriculum and inevitably imparts certain values, attitudes, and concepts about people and their world. Limited and stereotyped content, stilted sentence structure, and oversimplified plots do not lead to wholesome attitudes toward reading. To neglect interest and appeal in reading materials, is to discourage children from engaging in quantities of voluntary reading that will lead to a lifetime of reading.

Literature and Children. If one subscribes to the view that reading instruction should provide for personal and social growth while developing successful readers, then it is important to analyze the content of reading materials. Literature, to be enjoyed, must be interesting. Interests of children vary greatly according to age, sex, maturity level, previous experiences with books, previous life experiences, family level of education, and personal and cultural values. Materials designed to use and enrich existing interests of children and to develop new interests, therefore, are written around many themes and areas of human experience.

Traditionally, it has been assumed that a sequence derived from the social studies curriculum is suited to the developing interests of children. For this reason, content in reading materials at the primary level has dealt with immediate and personal experiences in the home and community. At the intermediate levels, themes have been extended to include people throughout the United States, the world, and other times. The middle-grade materials have placed increasing emphasis on literary materials and have included fanciful and folk tales and classical stories. Not until the seventh and eighth grades have social studies patterns disappeared from reading materials, with literary emphasis becoming predominant.

But reading interests of children are highly individual and personal. As boys and girls mature, their interests become even more varied and differentiated. Materials which ignore large segments of experience do not recognize children's varied literary interests, many of them awakened through the widespread viewing of television. Young children today show interest in topics as diversified as prehistoric times and outer space, the world of fantasy and the world of machines, and heroes, rascals, and knaves. Only materials which are geared to diversified interests and which provide stories dealing with a variety of exciting subjects can be evaluated as meeting the interests of children.

Just as the interests of children are varied, so are their needs. All children share one need, that of learning to read. Success or failure in reading is related closely to success or failure in school achievement, and eventually to the type of occupation one may enter. However, there are other needs which are highly individual and which may not be shared by many children. The need to understand one's self, one's motives, and one's social environment is universal; yet the particulars of each child's problems of personal and social development are unique. Each child finds different meaning and significance in content that appears to meet the general needs of children at each age level. For example, one may concede that all six-year olds need a sense of belonging. Yet the activities of the family portrayed in reading materials may alienate the child who lives in a housing project, who plays on the city streets, and whose father disappeared before he was born.

Purposes of children are varied, too. The child who wants to obtain information about stones may not be satisfied with a story about a lost doll. The child who is interested in something that happened last week in his community may not care about what happened to an Indian tribe in the southwest over a hundred years ago. When content is geared to concepts generally within the experience level of children, then it is matched to purposes of individual pupils only by chance. Children need help to discover the intellectual and personal satisfaction in asking real questions about their world, and finding answers through their reading. Whether this satisfaction should be obtained through the basic readers may be debated. If one believes it should be, then a variety of topics, subjects, and stories should be included in a complete reading program suited to the full range of pupil purposes.

Values are inevitably expressed in reading materials, whether or not the content is intended for that purpose. In studying children's readers, a group of psychologists at Yale University examined 914 simple narratives for implied values.* They concluded that stories in reading texts present unrealistic values to children. Although the content implies that effort and learning are rewarded, intellectual curiosity is not encouraged. Characters who ask for information are rewarded, but characters who try to figure out answers for themselves are punished. The narratives tell children how to achieve success but not how to take failure in stride. They provide models for achievement in boys; girls, however, are stereotyped as kind, but lacking in ambition and creativity. The stories appear to discourage independence while encouraging dependence.

---

* Lee J. Cronbach (ed.), *Text Materials in Modern Education* (Urbana, Ill.: University of Illinois Press, 1955), p. 36.

Critical Questions:

Do the materials appeal to and enrich existing varied interests of children?

Do the materials develop new interests?

Does the content include broad areas of human experience?

Is there a wide variety of content?

Is there balance among topics?

Do the materials appear suited to the background and experiences of the children who will use them?

Do the materials use language which the children in question readily understand (both vocabulary and manner of stating things)?

Do the materials contribute to the development of language abilities? If so, how?

Does the content lead to the devlopment of realistic attitudes and values?

Do the materials contribute to the development and broadening of tastes in literature?

Are the materials free from bias?

Do the materials appear to encourage increasing independence on the part of the reader? Is he led toward wider reading?

Has controversy been edited out of the materials, or are alternative points of view expressed?

Variety and Balance. A well-rounded program, many feel, provides materials for basic instruction in reading, for study-type reading in the content fields, for pleasurable reading, and for remedial or corrective instruction. Each of these categories in turn may be characterized by variety and balance. For example, a program planned to provide for pleasurable or recreational reading may include a wide variety of literary forms: nursery rhymes, picture stories, fables, folk tales, myths and legends, fantasy, heroes in epic and romance, biography, travel, history, fiction, and poetry. Or a well-designed program for teaching study-type reading may contain informational and expository materials in science, social studies, and health.

Other dimensions for determining variety in content include considerations of setting, style, characterization, and plot. Settings which expand horizons in time and place, help children understand their environment, and include vivid and descriptive language help to achieve variety and balance in reading.

A frequent criticism of reading materials is that style of writing is stilted. To a certain extent, this results from controls which limit vocabulary, length of sentences, length of lines, the number of pictures, and area of interest. Yet certain writers have been successful in overcoming the obstacles imposed by controls and have written in a more natural, flowing style characterized by beauty, pathos, and humor; plausible, direct coversation; and well-chosen figures of speech.

Characterization is important for the extension of experience through reading. Characters which are true-to-life provide children with the opportunity to assume the role of the hero. Identification increases the possibility that attitudes and values will develop out of reading. Strongly depicted, natural characters stimulate the reactions of pupils and contribute to a deeper understanding of personality, behavior, and motivation.

Plot, too, contributes to involving children emotionally in written materials. Well-knit and consistent plots with authentic outcomes are preferred by children. Trivial and obvious plots discourage children from responding enthusiastically to situations in stories that sometimes become needlessly repetitive.

Critical Questions:

Does the reading material present a variety of literary forms? Is there balance and variety in the settings, style, characterization, and plots of stories?

Are the materials suitable for children in all parts of the country, for inner-city, suburban, and rural children?

Is there balance between the new and the old, fact and fantasy, fictional and informational, humorous and serious?

Are the characters well drawn and true-to-life?

Are the plots well-knit and consistent?

Are informational materials such that vocabulary is extended, concepts developed, generalization encouraged, accuracy and authenticity assured? Are children aided in reading for information? Is the writing stilted, stiff, or artificial?

ARTISTIC QUALITY

Artistic quality is concerned with the appearance of reading materials, not primarily with the ideas contained in them. Educators vary in the importance they attach to artistic quality in reading materials. For some it is directly related to literary merit, while for others it is only indirectly related.

These differing points of view are exemplified by two statements of belief:

1. Reading materials should promote the aesthetic development of children. Some teachers and reading authorities hold that aesthetic development is a fundamental part of reading instruction. They believe that this important facet of the program must not be ignored. Learning and refining the basic reading skills ought to be accomplished in an environment that also fosters an understanding and appreciation of beauty.

2. Reading materials should be attractive to the children they are prepared for. If the artistic quality of the materials is high enough to draw children to them, the author and publisher have taken the first large step in motivating reading. When children want to use the materials, the instructional program is enhanced. The teacher can then concentrate on helping children use the materials appropriately rather than attempting to entice them to use the materials. The attractiveness of the materials is a key to reading interest.

Those who hold the first belief, with few exceptions, also hold the second. However, many who believe that reading materials should be attractive to children do not believe that the reading program per se should promote the aesthetic development of children. For this latter group, such understandings and appreciations are best developed in other portions of the school program; the reading program should focus on learning the basic reading skills. These two quite different positions are both widely held.

There is widespread agreement that the printed text is far more important than the artistic merit of the reading materials. Most school practitioners and reading authorities subscribe to the old saying, "don't judge a book by its cover." The materials may be quite attractive, but the ideas in the text may be of little interest or value to children. The reverse may also be true.

For the purpose of presenting and discussing principles that may be useful to analysts, artistic quality is arbitrarily divided into two categories: physical format and illustrations.

Physical format. The physical format of reading materials has received much attention and continuing attempts are made to increase its appeal. The reactions of children are very important. Analysts bring to their endeavors an understanding of what children's reactions are likely to be. The following questions may help the analyst utilize this understanding.

Is the appearance of the materials attractive? This question refers primarily to the cover of the book, workbook, or other materials: the outward appearance. Bright colors, appealing designs or pictures, interesting lettering, and engaging textures are factors in attracting children. Other factors are the size and, in some instances, the shape of the materials.

Is the print appropriate? If it is too large, children will reject the materials as beneath them. If it is too small, they will reject the materials as too difficult. Two factors other than size contribute to the appropriateness of print. They are the distance between lines of print and the width of margins. A cluttered page appears to have small print and gives the impression of difficult going.

Is page arrangement varied throughout the materials? Monotonous repetition of one arrangement decreases interest just as repetition of syle or content frequently causes children to "tune out." The "massing" of print, the blank or white areas, the placement of illustrations, and the use of color are all factors in page arrangement. They may be varied greatly to prevent monotony.

Is the paper substantial and of good quality? The paper used in the materials ought to be such that neither print nor illustrations can be seen through it. A dull finish is desirable to prevent glare. Most printed materials now have a cream or off-white paper. The binding needs to be strong enough for the repeated hard use school materials get.

Critical Questions:

Is the appearance of the materials attractive?

Is the print appropriate for the children who are to use the materials?

Is page arrangement varied throughout the materials? Is the paper substantial and of good quality? Is the material durably bound?

Illustrations. The drawings, photographs, charts, graphs, and designs that are included in reading materials may serve at least four functions. The first is providing direct assistance in developing basic reading skills. Many early reading materials are twice-told tales with the pictures telling the story at least as completely as the text. There is a growing body of evidence, however, that this is not as important as it was thought to be. Second, illustrations are a means of providing children with a common background; they supplement and extend the text of the materials. A third function served by illustrations is that of motivating children to read the materials. They may attract children and whet their interest. A fourth function is the use of illustrations to develop readiness. In the early grades readiness is promoted through illustrations as children improve in visual discrimination and perception of forms. In later grades this may be essentially a matter of obtaining necessary knowledge to understand and use the materials effectively.

Several questions may help guide analysts in critically examining the illustrations contained in reading materials:

Do the illustrations enrich the text? Many, but not all, authorities believe that illustrations used in reading materials should fit into the text so that children may gain from them additional meaning. In this view, text and illustrations are inseparable; each is supplemented by the other.

Are the illustrations appropriate to the children the materials are designed for? Younger children tend to be impressed by action and realism. Older children seem to be more receptive to detail, symbolism, and mood.

Do the illustrations create and mirror mood and feeling? Illustrations may build and maintain emotional settings. In certain reading materials, this use of illustrations is undesirable. Yet, it is known that where appropriate, design, color, and texture are important factors in developing and reflecting feeling.

Is character development portrayed convincingly? The illustrations included in reading materials can assist the text in building realistic characters, those that children enjoy and identify with. Imaginary characters can be quite realistic if they are convincingly portrayed in illustrations as well as text. On the other hand, characters may appear to be shallow and unreal if the illustrations are poor.

Are a variety of sizes, shapes, colors, and types of illustrations included in the reading materials? One purpose of illustrations is to attract children to the materials. Variety tends to promote interest. Another purpose of illustrations is to supplement the text. Not all ideas and feelings can most effectively be expressed in the same sort of illustration. Different approaches are necessary.

Is a portion of the illustrations reproductions of artistic masterpieces? Are there photographs of outstanding sculpture, architecture, and design? If reading materials should help develop an appreciation for the fine arts, these types of illustrations are important. These reproductions and photographs must be accurate in all details. A major difficulty often faced by authors and publishers is how to relate them to the text. Thus, these principles are hard to achieve.

Do the illustrations embody accepted principles of texture, shape and form, color, movement, and balance? Knowledge of these elements of artistic expression assists practitioners in determining the aesthetic quality of illustrations. Understanding and appreciation of design are affected by the examples available. Few would argue that producers of illustrations included in materials for children ought to ignore these principles. Attractiveness and appeal to children are very important considerations.

Are the illustrations in informational materials accurate and consistent with the text? Several other related questions that may be useful to analysts are: Is the information provided in the illustrations up-to-date? Are the illustrations pertinent to the ideas expressed in the text? Are the illustrations close enough to the related portions of the text for easy reference? Are important details clearly shown? Is size accurately presented?

Critical Questions:

Do the illustrations enrich the text?

Are the illustrations appropriate to the children the materials are designed for? Are they likely to be of interest to children?

Do the illustrations create and mirror mood and feeling?

Is character development portrayed convincingly?

Are a variety of sizes, shapes, colors, and types of illustrations included in the reading materials?

Are a portion of the illustrations reproductions of recognized artistic masterpieces? Are there photographs of outstanding sculpture, architecture, and design?

Do the illustrations embody accepted principles of texture, shape and form, color, movement, and balance?

Are the illustrations in informational materials accurate and consistent with the text? Is the information provided in the illustrations up-to-date? Are the illustrations pertinent to the ideas expressed in the text? Are the illustrations close enough to the related portions of the text for easy reference? Are important details clearly shown? Is size accurately presented?

SUMMARY

There is no consensus concerning the relevance of literary principles for analyzing reading materials. One view considers literary principles irrelevant to the materials used in teaching reading. Another view is that literary principles are relevant but less important than other considerations: reading materials are a special form of literature. In either view writing requires aesthetic value and artistic use of language before it is considered literature. When the goal of the instructional program is to teach children to read language for meaning, as in the second view, materials used in the program must be considered literature. Two categories of literary principles—content and artistic quality—are then important in analyzing and selecting the materials.

Literary principles in the content category arise from consideration of children's interests, needs, values, and purposes, and a concern for the variety and balance of literary styles and types. Principles in the category of artistic quality derive from study of physical format and illustrations.

Appendix

Critical Questions
for Analyzing and Selecting
Reading Materials

This list of critical questions will assist the school practitioner who must analyze and select reading texts and materials. The large number of questions in the list may bring to the attention of the analyst principles he has misunderstood, forgotten, or not known. They may extend his horizons and make him aware of the standards or criteria he applies and those he rejects.

Contained in each of the questions is a principle that may serve as a criterion or standard against which materials may be measured. The principles have been put in question form for clarity and greatest utility. Questions leading the analyst to look for certain characteristics assist in clearly focussing his examination of the materials.

This listing of critical questions is as inclusive as possible to provide all principles that might be considered important by the school practitioner. The omission of one or more principles is unintentional and does not in any way imply that such principles are unimportant or invalid, and no value judgment should be inferred from the fact that a principle appears in this list. This is an objective, comprehensive tabulation of principles that may help analysts of reading texts and materials.

No analyst will be able to use all the principles included in this list. He must decide which of the critical questions will most effectively guide his work. A list that is too

comprehensive is not only unwieldy but tends to place the
analyst in the position of searching for materials that will
be all things to all people. Some of the principles are
contradictory; the analyst must consciously choose which of
the conflicting principles he will use. He must also select
principles compatible with the philosophy of education and
concept of a good program of reading instruction that
guide his professional work. Finally, the principles he selects must be suitable to his classroom, school, and school
system. For maximum effectiveness he must make his choice
of principles thoughtfully and carefully. The principles the
analyst selects are the criteria or standard by which he
examines materials. This may mean that he will deliberately ignore whole sections, even categories, of critical questions because they have no relevance to his situation.

Research, common usage, and wide utility provide a
basis for grouping questions into categories and sections.
These groupings make it possible to use parts of the list
without combing the entire roster of questions. The relationship among the various questions is illuminated by this
arrangement.

Each question is numbered for easy reference. This
should not be construed as establishing a hierarchy of
importance. The relative emphasis accorded each principle
is the responsibility of the analyst. Occasionally, similar
questions appear in two or more places in the list. This
happens because certain topics legitimately belong in more
than one category. "Interest" is a good example.

Psychological Principles

CHILD DEVELOPMENT AND TEXTBOOK ORGANIZATION

1. Does the reading material reflect consideration of
child development?

2. Are the common characteristics of each age considered in the materials?
3. Do the materials emphasize differences or similarities?
4. Is physical maturation of children considered?
5. Are differences between interests and rate of development between boys and girls provided for?
6. Is there any attempt to correlate reading with other aspects of language development?
7. Is reading developed as a tool of learning in successively higher grades?

PLACEMENT OF READING SKILLS

8. How is the placement of reading skills determined?
9. How much and what kind of practice of reading skills is provided?
10. How is meaning handled in relation to reading skills in the first stages of reading instruction?
11. Is a stock of sight words taught before skill instruction is introduced?

CONTINUITY IN THE DEVELOPMENT OF SKILLS

12. Is skill instruction provided at appropriate times?
13. Is a planned sequence in skill instruction evident?
14. Is each skill presented in successively more difficult degrees?

COMPLETENESS OF SKILLS DEVELOPMENT

15. Are all necessary skills presented fully?
    –Phonics
    –Word recognition
    –Paragraph meaning
    –Vocabulary
    –Comprehension and interpretation
    –Spelling
    –Work-study

16. Which skills are emphasized and which are ignored or excluded?
17. Does the material meet the needs of all children?
18. What exclusions are made?

CONTENT TO BE READ

19. Does the content of successive units in the materials reflect general tendencies in children's personality development?
20. Is there a sequence from near to far?
21. Is there a sequence from now to then?
22. Is there a sequence from self to others?
23. Is there a sequence from the family to larger social units?
24. Are plots involving frustration and anxiety avoided in early grades?
25. Does the content reflect the increased vicarious experience of modern children?
26. Are nonfiction materials included to tap the broader interest of today's children?

PERSONALITY GROWTH THROUGH READING

27. Does the material extend the experience of the reader?
28. Does the content help the learner understand himself and the world?
29. Does the material insure success to the child in early stages? In later stages?
30. How is success provided?
31. Are efforts made to stimulate children to read widely outside school?

READINESS

32. Are readiness activities provided in the beginning materials and/or throughout the program to develop

language fluency, motor skills, and recognition of shape, form, and sounds?

33. Are readiness workbooks provided?
34. Is help provided to the teacher in identifying and developing readiness?
35. Does the material differentiate between teaching level and independent reading level?
36. Is aid given the learner to make it possible for him to learn independently?
37. Are skills and facts presented and taught as prerequisite learning before reading may take place: the alphabet, phonic skills, sight words, grapheme-phoneme correspondences?

MOTIVATION AND INTEREST

38. Are motivational devices and activities built into the materials?
39. Is help provided for the teacher to achieve general and specific motivation for learning?
40. Are the design, format, pictures, and other aspects sufficiently attractive to motivate interest?
41. Is the child's satisfaction of his needs the basis for motivation?
42. Does the reading material employ a variety of enrichment activities for motivation?
43. Do the materials create a desire to know in pupils: do they arouse curiosity, capitalize on children's interests and concerns, and provide needed knowledge about the world around them?
44. Does the material tap the motivational aspects of the child's own sub-culture?
45. Do the materials and the suggestions for use make children feel worthy and accepted?
46. Does the content utilize literary techniques to provide

excitement, involvement, suspense, humor, and other sources of interest?

OTHER LEARNING PRINCIPLES

47. Is a theory of learning stated or implied in the material? What is it?

48. Is the material consistent with a stated or implied theory of learning?

49. Is the teacher helped to understand and apply the theory of learning?

50. Does the material prepare the child for learning by arousing interest, helping him acquire a mental set for learning, presenting him with a background adequate for the new learning, and preparing him to take action or respond in some way?

51. Does the material create "an appropriate" or "manageable level of anxiety" or curiosity within the child so that his attention is focused on the stimulus or problem to be solved?

52. Is the material presented in such a way as to provide the learner with auditory as well as visual stimuli? Can the child learn to bring to the printed word the same response pattern he has previously brought to the spoken word?

53. Does the material permit the child to draw on his fund of meaning so that he can integrate new meanings with the old?

54. Does the material permit the child to systematize or organize his knowledge or to acquire insight?

55. Does the material permit the child to use his learning actively in new situations or to generalize his learnings?

56. Does the material permit the child to complete a task and avoid the confusion of inadequate learning?

57. Does the material provide distributed practice rather than massed practices in the learning of skills and abilities?

Sociocultural Principles

WHAT CHILDREN LIKE TO READ

58. To what extent do the materials reflect the reading interests of children of the age and sex and background they were designed for?
59. Do the materials extend and develop a rich variety of reading interests? If so, how?
60. Are provisions made for meeting the interests of both boys and girls? In what way is this done?
61. How are differences in interests related to intelligence and socioeconomic background provided for?

SOCIAL CLASS AND EXPERIENCE

62. Is the content of the reading materials appropriate to the social class background of the children who use them? Does it make sense to them? Is content an important aspect of the program espoused by the authors of the materials? Is the content familiar to the children? Are they likely to relate it to what they have experienced?
63. To what extent do the materials promote a desire to read? How is this handled?
64. Are social classes characterized accurately?
65. Are story settings common ones for the readers?
66. How do the materials help prepare children for new learnings that are yet to come? Are there provisions for developing readiness?
67. How do the materials contribute to expanding the experiential background of children?

DIALECT DIFFERENCES

68. Is there a recognition of and provision for dialect differences in the materials? If so, how is it handled? Will some children be unduly penalized by the language patterns used?

69. Are the materials designed for one dialect group or for all children? If the former, is the dialect presented accurately?

70. In materials based on phonic or linguistic principles, are differences in pronunciation possible and acceptable?

71. Are the idioms included in the materials appropriate to the level of understanding and dialect of the children who will use them?

72. Is slang used in the materials? If so, is it up-to-date, appropriate, and meaningful to the children who will use the materials?

73. Do the materials introduce the dominant language pattern consistently and accurately?

74. Are words and phrases with special meaning or double entendre in some dialects handled carefully?

ROLE DEVELOPMENT

75. Are the activities engaged in by story characters appropriate of the roles usually ascribe to them in the general culture?

76. Are appropriate models for behavior in the materials?

77. With whom do the story characters associate?

78. What is the constituency of the family group? What is the pattern of relationships within the family?

79. Is the story setting predominantly urban, rural, or suburban? Are the roles pictured realistically and accurately in these settings?

80. What occupations are shown and how are they represented? Are a variety included? Are hidden value judgments a part of the presentation?
81. How are story characters dressed?

VALUES

82. What values are intentionally presented? Are the values of the general culture reflected in the reading materials?
83. Are the values expressed portrayed in a positive manner? If so, do they tend to stimulate appreciation and acceptance?
84. Are negative values expressed in such a manner as to encourage rejection? Would the material incidentally develop undesirable values?
85. Do the values expressed complement the known values of the group the materials are intended for? Do characters act in ways which fit a desirable value structure? Are values presented with too heavy a hand? Do the materials preach too much? Is assistance given to the teacher in identifying values presented and following up on these values?

Educational Principles

SEQUENCE, SCOPE, AND INTEGRATION

86. Do the reading materials provide continuity of growth in reading skills, habits, and attitudes? How?
87. Do the reading materials provide for a wide variety of reading activities? In what way?
88. Is a complete organization of reading experiences provided?
89. Do the reading materials provide for a worthwhile content by ideas? How?

90. Do the reading materials embody vocabulary controls? If so, are the basic words appropriate to the needs and interests of children?

91. Is the number of basic words sufficient to provide enough story to retain the interest of children?

92. Is the amount of repetition sufficient to ensure retention? Is it likely to repel children?

93. Do words recur throughout the book or series or do they tend to be presented intensively at one point and then not used again?

94. Are meaning and recognition of words developed together?

95. Do the materials contain phonic controls? If so, what portion of the materials are devoted to phonics?

96. To what extent do phonics constitute a formal, systematic program of instruction?

97. How is phonics integrated with other aspects of the reading program?

98. Are the phonics principles clearly and accurately presented?

99. Do the reading materials include linguistic controls? If so, does the language structure in the reading materials move from simple to more complex?

100. Is the level of complexity appropriate to the abilities of the children the materials were prepared for?

101. Are commonly used patterns of language employed in the materials?

102. Do the reading materials employ concept controls? If so, is the concept load sufficiently restricted in materials prepared for use in the early stages of the instructional program, so that children may concentrate on mastering basic reading skills?

103. Are concepts smoothly and reasonably developed and extended in the reading materials?
104. Is the concept level of the content appropriate to the children who are to use the reading materials?
105. Do the reading materials embody interest controls? If so, do the materials parallel what is known about the reading interests of the children they are designed for?
106. Are the materials designed to develop new interests in children?
107. Do the reading materials include literary controls? If so, is the content of high literary quality?
108. Is the content tastefully and artistically presented?
109. Do the materials contain a variety of literary forms?

LEGIBILITY

110. Is the type size appropriate for the developmental stage of the children the materials are designed for?
111. Does the kind of type interfere with legibility?
112. Is the distance between lines of print within the range recommended for ease of reading?
113. Are the length of lines of print within the known range of preferences?
114. Is the reflection of light by the pages of the materials reduced to a minimum?

ASSOCIATED LEARNINGS

115. Is the informational content relevant to the experiences of the pupils the materials are designed for?
116. Is the information contained in the materials adequate for these children?
117. Is the information clearly and accurately presented?
118. Are the vocabulary and concepts suitable to the age

and interest level of the pupils and to the subject matter of the text?

119. Are explanations of technical terms or unfamiliar words necessary to the content provided as they are introduced?

SUITABILITY

120. Are the stated or implicit purposes, goals, or objectives of the materials compatible with the point of view of the adopting school?

121. Are the materials themselves in harmony with policies of the school?

122. Are all facets of the reading program covered?

123. Are the materials more economical than others that are available?

124. Are the materials based upon the findings of sound research conducted in situations similar to that for which they are being considered for adoption?

125. Are the reading materials correlated with the texts and materials in other areas of study?

TEACHABILITY

To what extent do the reading materials provide for:

126. Continuing the cultivation of readiness for new levels of skill development?

127. Building a larger reading vocabulary?

128. Developing greater skill in identifying unfamiliar words?

129. Giving impetus to wider reading beyond the basal materials?

130. Discovering and eliminating reading deficiencies?

131. Measuring pupil achievement?

132. Meeting individual differences in ability, skill, need, and interest of children?

133. Do the materials supply a wide variety of selections and materials for pupils?

134. To what extent do the materials furnish adequate, clear, instructional suggestions as well as a coherent, valid pattern of suggested method that teachers might find helpful?

Linguistic Principles

ACCURACY OF LANGUAGE INFORMATION

135. What language information is provided for the teacher?

136. Is language information provided for direct instruction to the pupil?

137. Are exercises provided which confirm or present language information?

138. What is the source of language information?

139. Is the language information presented consistent within itself?

140. Is the language information presented consistent with scientific knowledge of language?

PHONEMIC CONSIDERATIONS

141. What provision is made for controlling grapheme-phoneme correspondence?

142. Is this provision consistent throughout the materials?

143. Is irregularity introduced in a planned and systematic way?

144. Are spelling patterns used in building the materials?

145. Are spelling patterns used consistently?

146. Are phonics (sound-symbol) generalizations taught as such in the materials?

MORPHEMIC CONSIDERATIONS

147. What focus is there in the reading material on words as such?
148. Is any assistance offered to the pupil in delineating words and developing a concept of what words are?
149. Are words presented and taught in isolation? If so, how are the problems of intonation and pronunciation handled?
150. What attention is given to compound words?
151. How are inflectional and derivational suffixes handled in the material?
152. Are contractions used in places where adults would normally use them, or are contractions avoided?

SYNTACTIC CONSIDERATIONS

153. Is the language of the reading material real language, similar to the oral language as the learner knows it?
154. Do reading materials contain the common language structures of oral language?
155. Do these structures occur in the same frequency as in oral language?
156. Is any attempt made to proceed from common to uncommon language structures?
157. Is any attempt made to proceed from simple to complex fillers of the slots in language structures?
158. Are structural and contextual ambiguity avoided?
159. How are function words handled in reading material?
160. Are there any special efforts in the reading material to present syntactic cues in reading?
161. Is any special effort made in teacher materials to assist him in helping children to use syntactic cues?

INTONATION CONSIDERATIONS

162. Do the reading materials relate punctuation to intonation?
163. Are children encouraged to supply the natural intonations in reading?
164. Does the material assist the teacher in understanding how intonation functions in communication?
165. Does the material assist the teacher in helping children achieve natural intonations?

DIALECT CONSIDERATIONS

166. Do the reading materials assume a single "correct" English?
167. Do the materials for the teacher and the child separate learning to read from learning a preferred dialect?
168. Are dialect differences recognized? How?
169. Is there provision for dialect differences in the materials? How?
170. Is any attempt made to change oral language: prior to reading instruction; concurrently with reading instruction?
171. Is there any attempt to widen the range of language comprehension and use?
172. What assistance, if any, is given the teacher in understanding dialect problems in reading?

GENERAL LINGUISTIC CONSIDERATIONS

173. Is the reading material based on child language?
174. Does the reading material reflect the view that language learning is developmental?
175. Is the teacher provided with help in understanding child language and child language development?

176. Does the material draw on the prior language knowledge of the learners?
177. Does the material help the teacher draw on the prior language knowledge of the learner?
178. What definition of reading is stated or implicit in the reading materials?
179. Are early reading materials meaningful?
180. If so, is the meaning within the range of experience and conceptual development of the learners?
181. Are pictures used to cue meaning?
182. Are skills implicitly or explicitly regarded as ends or means in the materials?
183. Is redundancy considered in constructing the material?
184. Do the reading materials correspond in redundancy to the oral language of children?

Literary Principles

READING MATERIALS NOT LITERATURE

185. Is the reading material based on a view of reading instruction in which literary principles are relevant?

INSTRUCTIONAL MATERIALS AS A SPECIAL FORM OF LITERAURE

186. Are instructional reading materials viewed as a special form of literature?
187. Are literary qualities of the content ends in themselves or means to facilitate learning of skills?

LITERATURE AND CHILDREN

188. Do the materials appeal to and enrich existing varied interests of children?
189. Do the materials develop new interest?

190. Does the content include broad areas of human experience?
191. Is there a wide variety of content?
192. Is there balance among topics?
193. Do the materials appear suited to the background and experiences of the children who will use them?
194. Do the materials use language which the children in question readily understand (both vocabulary and manner of stating things)?
195. Do the materials contribute to the development of language abilities? If so, how?
196. Does the content lead to the development of realistic attitudes and values?
197. Do the materials contribute to the development and broadening of tastes in literature?
198. Are the materials free from bias?
199. Do the materials appear to encourage increasing independence on the part of the reader? Is he led toward wider reading?
200. Has controversy been edited out of the materials, or are alternative points of view expressed?

VARIETY AND BALANCE

201. Does the reading material present a variety of literary forms? Is there balance and variety in the settings, style, characterization, and plots of stories?
202. Are the materials suitable for children in all parts of the country, for inner-city, suburban, and rural children?
203. Is there balance between the new and the old, fact and fantasy, fictional and informational, humorous and serious?
204. Are the characters well drawn and true-to-life?
205. Are the plots well-knit and consistent?

206. Are informational materials such that vocabulary is extended, concepts developed, generalization encouraged, accuracy and authenticity assured? Are children aided in reading for information? Is the writing stilted, stiff, or artificial?

PHYSICAL FORMAT

207. Is the appearance of the materials attractive?
208. Is the print appropriate for the children who are to use the materials?
209. Is page arrangement varied throughout the material?
210. Is the paper substantial and of good quality? Is the material durably bound?

ILLUSTRATIONS

211. Do the illustrations enrich the text?
212. Are the illustrations appropriate to the children the materials are designed for? Are they likely to be of interest to children?
213. Do the illustrations create and mirror mood and feeling?
214. Is character development portrayed convincingly?
215. Are a variety of sizes, shapes, colors, and types of illustrations included in the reading materials?
216. Are a portion of the illustrations reproductions of recognized artistic masterpieces? Are there photographs of outstanding sculpture, architecture, and design?
217. Do the illustrations embody accepted principles of texture, shape and form, color, movement, and balance?
218. Are the illustrations in informational materials accurate and consistent with the text? Is the information provided in the illustrations up-to-date? Are the illus-

trations pertinent to the ideas expressed in the text? Are the illustrations close enough to the related portions of the text for easy reference? Are important details clearly shown? Is size accurately presented?

Selected

Bibliography

Arbuthnot, May H. *Children and Books*. Chicago: Scott, Foresman & Company, 1964.

Throughout the book there are guidelines for good literature. The author discusses types of literature, interests of children, graphic representations, and criteria for evaluating materials for children.

Bloomfield, Leonard and Clarence Barnhart. *Let's Read, A Linguistic Approach*. Detroit: Wayne State University Press, 1961.

Bloomfield actually produced the material and method in this book some thirty years ago. He taught his own children to read using letter-sound regularity; the principle is one letter for one sound. Barnhart edited this several years after Bloomfield's death.

Carroll, John B. "The Analysis of Reading Instruction: Perspectives from Psychology and Linguistics," *Theories of Learning and Instruction*, Sixty-third Yearbook of the National Society for the Study of Education, Part I. (Chicago: University of Chicago Press, 1964) ,pp. 336–53.

Carrol applies psychology and linguistics to how reading instruction may be studied and understood.

Cronbach, Lee J. (ed.). *Text Materials in Modern Education*. Urbana, Ill.: University of Illinois Press, 1955.

A balanced examination of the contributions of text materials to learning and the course of study, with an emphasis on theoretical considerations regarding selection and evaluation.

Dechant, Emerald V. *Improving the Teaching of Reading.* Englewood Cliffs, N. J.: Prentice-Hall, Inc., 1964.

Materials for use in reading instruction are listed, described, and classified. Provides an introduction to the range of reading materials available.

Fries, Charles C. *Linguistics and Reading.* New York: Holt, Rinehart & Winston, Inc., 1963.

This book by one of America's leading linguists has several important features: a very fine review of methods of teaching reading; a good simple overview of linguistics; and what Fries calls, "The essentials of a linguistically sound approach." This last is a proposal to base teaching of reading on contrasting spelling patterns.

Goodman, Kenneth S. "A Communicative Theory of the Reading Curriculum," *Elementary English* (March 1963), pp. 290–98.

The author presents a partial theory of reading based on linguistic insights.

————. "The Linguistics of Reading," *Elementary School Journal,* 64 (April 1964), 355–61.

This is a summary of what linguistics can and cannot do for the teaching of reading.

Gray, William S. (ed.). *Promoting Personal and Social Development through Reading,* Supplementary Educational Monographs, No. 64. Chicago: University of Chicago Press, 1947.

In this monograph, Gray has brought together a collection of articles concerned with promoting personal and social development. Areas directly related to personal development are: personal well-being, understanding people, knowledge of the natural world, and aesthetic and spiritual values. Social development is promoted through reading about our democratic patterns of life, the current social scene, intergroup understandings, and international understanding. A number of values are identified and the effects of reading on the development of these values are suggested.

Huck, Charlotte S. and Doris A. Young. *Children's Literature in the Elementary School.* New York: Holt, Rinehart, & Winston, Inc., 1961.

The authors provide a good overview of literature for elementary school children. The reading interests of children are discussed, and suggestions for analyzing and selecting materials are presented.

Lefevre, Carl A. *Linguistics and the Teaching of Reading.* New York: McGraw-Hill Book Co., 1964.

Lefevre presents an approach to reading which focuses on large language units, sentences, and sequences of sentences. In Lefevre's view, every reading teacher must know linguistics. His book provides a very good overview of the linguistics teachers need to know.

National Society for the Study of Education. *Development in and through Reading,* Sixtieth Yearbook, Part I. Chicago: University of Chicago Press, 1961.

The yearbook emphasizes the developmental aspects of reading instruction with special attention to the roles of motive, need, and interest.

Robinson, Helen M. (ed.). *Developing Permanent Interest in Reading,* Supplementary Educational Monographs, No. 84. Chicago: University of Chicago Press, 1956.

The reading interests of children at several age levels are discussed. Goals, methods, and materials of instruction for improving interests, and the effects of mass media are explored. The role of the content areas in extending reading interests is examined. The final section is devoted to administrative procedures for developing reading instruction.

Russell, David H. *Children Learn to Read,* 2nd ed. Boston: Ginn and Company, 1961.

This book contains a useful discussion of materials that

might be included in a reading program. The relationship between reading materials and techniques of teaching reading is explored. Many ways are suggested for providing, using, and housing reading materials.

Seagoe, May V. *A Teacher's Guide to the Learning Process.* Dubuque, Iowa: William C. Brown Company, 1961.

A practical approach to the improvement of teaching from the standpoint of the teacher and questions of procedure in the classroom.

Traxler, Arthur E. and Ann Jungeblut. *Resarch in Reading during Another Four Years,* Educational Records Bulletin, No. 75. New York: Educational Records Bureau, 1960.

Research in reading from 1953 to 1957 is reported in twenty-one categories. Of particular interest are the studies in the areas of reading and personal and social adjustment, reading interests, and developmental reading. An extensive annotated bibliography of selected studies in each of these areas assists the reader in locating pertinent articles, books, and reading bibliographies.

Warner, W. Lloyd. *Social Class in America.* Chicago: Science Research Associates, Inc., 1949.

Social class structure in America is examined in detail. The methodology of the study is described. The tools and techinques of the researcher are described. Six levels of social class are identified and characterized using a carefully constructed scale. Each of the classes is discussed in detail and the implications of knowledge of what social class is and how it works are presented.

Index

Accuracy, of concepts, 75; of information, 83; of language information, 95

Alphabet, 94, 113; initial teaching alphabet (ITA), 98

Appearance, 78, 123

Attitudes, 41, 46, 47, 116

Betts, Emmett A., 30

Characters, as behavior models, 57, 59; development of in stories, 125

Child development, 22–24; aesthetic, 121; ideolect, 42; language acquisition, 100, 101, 108, 109; personality, 28; physical maturation, 24; relationship to achievement, 25; role, 41, 58, 60; self-concept, 41; sequence, 28; stages, 22

Communication, 89; theory, 90, 110

Comprehension, 27

Concepts, 74–76; accuracy of, 75; complexity, 74, 75; concept burden, 75; conceptual controls, 74–76; definition of, 74; determining level, 76; interest and, 83; suitability, 83

Content, reading, 27, 85; experience stories, 102, 111; interest in, 82, 83; relationship to personality development, 28, 29

Context, 38; as aid in learning 38, 39; picture, 110; syntactic, 101; units of meaning, 39; words in, 102, 103

Controls, compatibility, 71; concept, 74–76; interest, 76–77; linguistic, 73, 74; literary, 77, 78; phonics, 72; use of, 70, 71; validity of, 71; vocabulary, 71, 72, 109, 110

Contractions, 100

Correlation, with other materials, 86

Dechant, Emerald V., 80

Dialect, 42; and correctness, 106; and ideolect, 53; and spelling, 105, 106; approaches to, 106; considerations, 105–7; differences, 52–56; idioms, 53, 54; slang, 53, 54

Dictionary, use, 72

Drill, 33; vocabulary, 72

Economy, 85

Experience, 46–52, 75–76; experience stories, 102, 111; child's world, 28; vicarious, 28

Expression. *See* Intonation

Factual materials, 69

Failure, 29

Fiction, 69

Format, 122; appearance, 78, 123; artistic quality, 121; page arrangement, 123; paper, 123; print, 123

Fries, Charles C., 98
Function words. *See* Words

Graphemes, 94, 113; grapheme-
phoneme correspondence, 94,
97, 98

Harris, Albert J., 27
Herrick, Virgil E., 26
Hollingshead, August B., 47

Illustrations, 124–26
Individual differences, 31; interests, 42–46; range of reaching
ability, 31; variations in speech,
31; variations in learning pattern, 31
Individualizing instruction, 32;
teacher's responsibility, 32;
some provision by publisher, 32
Inflection, 92; acquisition of
suffixes, 100
Information, 69; adequacy, 83;
and interest, 83; presentation
of, 83; language, 95; relevancy,
82, 83
Initial teaching alphabet (ITA),
98
Instruction, levels of, 33; large
group approach, 31; methods
(combined), 31; sequence of,
26; whole word views, 98
Integration, 68–70
Interest, 21, 23–24, 28, 35, 36, 41,
77, 115–17; and content, 82, 83;
controls, 76, 77; correlation of
materials, 86; development of,
77; individual differences in,
42–64
Interpretation, 27
Intonation, 93, 94; and punctuation, 104; considerations, 104,
105; in words, 99, 100; terminals
in, 104

Language, 89; abilities, 24; accuracy of information, 95; acquisition of, 100, 101, 108, 109; child,
73, 74, 102, 107, 108; common
patterns, 41,42, 73, 74, 92, 102;
complexity of, 73; controls, 73,
74; development, 22; expansion
of, 107; real, 74
Learning, behaviorist theories, 37;
faculty psychology, 37; field
theory, 37; Gestalt, 37; habit
formation theory, 38; language,
23, 24, 100, 101, 108, 109; reinforcement, 38; skill development, 69, 74, 75, 82, 87
Legibility, 80–82; definition, 80;
length of lines, 81; type size,
80
Linguistics, 89–112; controls, 73,
74; definition, 73, 89; descriptive, 90; terminology, 90–95
Literary controls, 77, 78; devices,
115; quality, 115
Literature, 113; characterization
in, 120; form, 115; plot, 120;
setting, 120; type, 115
Loban, Walter, 101

Magazines, 49
Mead, George, 59
Meaning, 25, 27, 72, 74, 75, 92;
and pictures, 110; and syntax,
101; contextual units, 30, 39; in
early materials, 109; patterns of
thought, 30
Methods. *See* Instruction
Morphemes, bound, 92; considerations, 99–101; definition, 91, 92;
free, 91; plurals, 100
Motivation, 34, 35

Newspapers, 48, 49

Oral language, pauses in, 99; patterns in, 54, 101

Phonemes, 113; considerations, 97–99; definition, 91; grapheme-phoneme correspondence, 94, 97, 98; phonemics, 95; sequences, 110

Phonics, 27, 113; controls, 72; definition, 72; linguist's views, 97, 98

Poetry, 69

Pictures and meaning, 110

Preston, Ralph C., 30

Principles, educational defined, 68 organization of, 20, 21; psychological, 22; selection of, 13, 18

Print, 123, 80, 81; length of lines, 81; type size, 80

Problem solving, 38

Pronunciation, 100

Psycholinguistics, 90, 100

Punctuation, 94; and intonation, 104

Readiness, 32; and workbooks, 32

Reading, definitions of, 89; interests, 42–46, 83; recreational, 69; voluntary, 30

Reading materials, analysis of, 17, 19, 20; ease of use, 80–82; scope, 68–70; selection of, 16; sequence, 68–70; suitability of, 84; types of, 15, 70; variety in, 78, 85

Reading skills, 25; completeness, 26, 27; placement, 25, 26; practice, 25; sequence, 25, 26; speed, 80–82; word attacks, 27; work-study, 27

Redundancy, 110, 111

Repetition, 71

Research findings, use of, 85, 86

Role, development of, 41, 56, 60; sociocultural influences on, 56–62

Russell, David H., 24

Self-concept, 30, 41

Sentence. *See* Syntax

Sight vocabulary. *See* Word recognition

Skinner, B. F., 38

Slang. *See* Dialect

Social class, 46–50; characteristics, 47–50

Sociocultural influences, 41; role, 56–62

Sociological forces, 34

Speech. *See* Oral language

Spelling, 27; and dialect, 105, 106; function words, 93; patterns, 98, 99

Strickland, Ruth, 101

Success in reading, 29, 30

Suffixes, inflectional and derivational, 100

Syllables, nonsense, 97

Syntax, agreement on, 95; considerations, 101–4; defined, 92; markers, 93; patterns, 41–42, 101; sentence, 104

Taba, Hilda, 37

Technical terms, 83, 84

Values, 41, 46, 47, 63–66, 116, 118

Vocabulary, 27, 100; controlled, 71, 72, 109, 110; growth, 23, 83, 87

Warner, W. Lloyd, 47

Word attack, 27

Word recognition, 23, 26, 27, 69, 71

Words, allologues, 100; and morphemes, 92; function or structure, 92, 93, 103; intonation in, 99, 100; in context, 102, 103; "s" forms, 100; whole word views, 98

Workbooks, 32

The book was designed by Sylvia Winter.
The text typeface is Baskerville originally
cut by John Baskerville in the 18th Century.
The display face is Century Schoolbook based on
a face originally cut by Linn B. Benton
in the late 19th Century.
The book is printed on Warren's Olde Style
Antique and bound in Holliston Mills'
Kingston cloth over boards.
Manufactured in the United States of America.

Kenneth S. Goodman, Hans C. Olsen, Jr., Cynthia M.
Colvin, and Louis F. VanderLinde are associate professors
of elementary education at Wayne State University.

16. Which skills are emphasized and which are ignored or excluded?
17. Does the material meet the needs of all children?
18. What exclusions are made?

CONTENT TO BE READ

19. Does the content of successive units in the materials reflect general tendencies in children's personality development?
20. Is there a sequence from near to far?
21. Is there a sequence from now to then?
22. Is there a sequence from self to others?
23. Is there a sequence from the family to larger social units?
24. Are plots involving frustration and anxiety avoided in early grades?
25. Does the content reflect the increased vicarious experience of modern children?
26. Are nonfiction materials included to tap the broader interest of today's children?

PERSONALITY GROWTH THROUGH READING

27. Does the material extend the experience of the reader?
28. Does the content help the learner understand himself and the world?
29. Does the material insure success to the child in early stages? In later stages?
30. How is success provided?
31. Are efforts made to stimulate children to read widely outside school?

READINESS

32. Are readiness activities provided in the beginning materials and/or throughout the program to develop

2. Are the common characteristics of each age considered in the materials?
3. Do the materials emphasize differences or similarities?
4. Is physical maturation of children considered?
5. Are differences between interests and rate of development between boys and girls provided for?
6. Is there any attempt to correlate reading with other aspects of language development?
7. Is reading developed as a tool of learning in successively higher grades?

PLACEMENT OF READING SKILLS

8. How is the placement of reading skills determined?
9. How much and what kind of practice of reading skills is provided?
10. How is meaning handled in relation to reading skills in the first stages of reading instruction?
11. Is a stock of sight words taught before skill instruction is introduced?

CONTINUITY IN THE DEVELOPMENT OF SKILLS

12. Is skill instruction provided at appropriate times?
13. Is a planned sequence in skill instruction evident?
14. Is each skill presented in successively more difficult degrees?

COMPLETENESS OF SKILLS DEVELOPMENT

15. Are all necessary skills presented fully?
    –Phonics
    –Word recognition
    –Paragraph meaning
    –Vocabulary
    –Comprehension and interpretation
    –Spelling
    –Work-study